100 Children's Club Activities

'We will tell the next generation.'
(Psalm 78:4)

100 Children's Club Activities

Jan Dyer

Eastbourne

First published 2001
New edition 2006
1 2 3 4 5 6 7 Printing/Year 09 08 07 06

ISBN – 10: 1 84291 289 5
ISBN – 13: 978 1 842912 89 8

*Illustrations based on cartoons by
Rebekah and Hannah Dyer*

Designed by PinnacleCreative.co.uk

Published by
Kingsway Communications Ltd
Lottbridge Drove, Eastbourne BN23 6NT, England.
Email: childrensministry@kingsway.co.uk

Printed in the USA

CONTENTS

Acknowledgements 11
Introduction 12

PART ONE
Start Here 17
The Story of One Group 35
More Approaches 38
Using This Book to Plan a Session 42

PART TWO
SECTION ONE: ICEBREAKERS
1. Space flight 50
2. In the river, on the bank 53
3. Choose a colour 55
4. Human noughts and crosses 57
5. Pass the parcel / Arnold says 59
6. Ring on a string 62
7. Pass the sock 64
8. Parachute crossovers 66
9. Parachute football / popcorn 68
10. Parachute cat and mouse / sharks 70

SECTION TWO: CRAFT ACTIVITIES
11. Making caterpillars 74
12. Using play dough 76
13. Clay modelling 78
14. Modelling with coloured clay 82
15. Animal masks 84
16. Colouring a picture 86
17. Making a mural 88
18. Rubbings 90
19. Making mats 94
20. Paint a letter 96
21. Painting on wood 98

22. Tie dye 100
23. Pebble paperweights 102
24. Making bead jewellery 104
25. Acetate greetings cards 106
26. Painting mugs and plates 108

SECTION THREE: FOOD ACTIVITIES
27. Marshmallow pigs 112
28. Making sweets 114
29. Making jelly ponds 116
30. Icing biscuits and buns 118
31. Making edible jewellery 120
32. Making sandwiches 122
33. Making fruit salad 124
34. Making popcorn 126
35. Making biscuits 128
36. Making bread rolls 130
37. Making bread without yeast 132
38. Making pizza 134
39. Growing cress heads 136

SECTION FOUR: ENERGETIC GAMES
40. Relay races 140
41. Bun relay 143
42. Bangers and mash 145
43. Have you got it? 147
44. Shoes and pans 149
45. Football, uni-hockey and basketball 151
46. Obstacle course 153
47. Pass the ball 155
48. Stop and go 157
49. Cat and mouse 159

SECTION FIVE: NOT-SO-ENERGETIC GAMES
50. Catching bugs / fish 162
51. Guess who / Follow the leader 165
52. Do you fit? 167
53. 'Caw, raven, caw' 169

54. Still lions / Lions' stalk 171
55. In size order 174
56. Shoe sizes 176
57. Snail race 178
58. Follow your elbow / Are you a nose? 180
59. Flap the fish 183

SECTION SIX: PARTY GAMES AND CHALLENGES
60. Pick a pea 188
61. Ping-pong race 190
62. Jelly slurp / saucer of milk 192
63. Pinning the tail on the donkey 194
64. Twister 196
65. Feed your partner 198
66. Find the sweet 200
67. Catch the apple 202
68. Pinball / table football 204

SECTION SEVEN: TELLING STORIES
69. Dramatised story 1. You the Storyteller 208
70. Dramatised story 2. Using words and actions 210
71. An active story 212
72. Using puppets 213
73. Puppet dialogue 214
74. Using puppets in story review 216
75. Telling a story using colours 219
76. Telling a story using flags 222
77. Telling a story using a parachute 225
78. Telling a story using hidden objects 228
79. Telling stories using dance drama 230
80. Reading stories 233
81. Telling a story using a video 235
82. Telling a story using quizzes 237

SECTION EIGHT: PRAYER AND PRAISE
83. Using songs 242
84. Using puppets 244
85. Using percussion instruments 246

86. Praise with a parachute 249
87. Prayer with a parachute 251
88. Saying 'sorry' with a parachute 253
89. Bounce or roll a prayer 255
90. Using dance 257
91. Using flags and ribbons 260
92. Using rap 262
93. Using prayer books 264
94. Pass the Beanie 265
95. Prayer partners 266
96. Praying for the family 267
97. Flying prayers 268
98. Prayer consequences 270
99. Folding a cross 272
100. Using balloons 274

PART THREE

Flags and Ribbons 279
Parachutes 281
Play Dough Recipe 283
Resources 285
Useful Addresses 289

Scripture Index 293
Subject Index 295

ACKNOWLEDGEMENTS

A big thank you to my husband Graham and to our children, Rachel, Hannah and Rebekah, for all their support and encouragement in the writing of this book. The family have 'lived' the book as it has been written and have shared in the bouncing of ideas. They have also found themselves cooking more meals, ironing more clothes and getting more practice in cleaning the house. This I have appreciated, together with their sacrifice of computer time for their own assignments and leisure activities. Further thanks to Hannah and Rebekah for their illustrations and to Graham for idea 82.

I would also like to thank the children at BUGZ (Building Up God's Zone) meeting midweek at Christ Church, Lye, who have been the inspiration for this book, and the children of the 'A' and 'B' Teams in Sheffield who have shared their ideas with me. Also to the Blitz After School Club and 323 Club from the WEC, Walsall, Kids Quest at Amblecote Christian Centre and Mini Soccer 4–4–2 from Christ Church, Lye, for their contributions to 'More Approaches'.

The ideas in this book have been used in BUGZ or in the 'A' and 'B' Teams in Sheffield. The reader will be aware that some of the ideas are adaptations of games and activities that have been passed down from one generation of children to another, and thus I do not know their original source.

Thank you, too, to the many friends who have been praying for me as I have been writing this book – for their support and encouragement, and for so patiently waiting for that cup of coffee we have been looking forward to having together. Finally, thank you to Nichola and Angela for their reading of parts of the manuscript and their constructive comments, and to the children's leaders around the country who have talked to me about their groups and encouraged me to write this book.

INTRODUCTION

This book is written with the expectation that Christian teaching is integral to your children's club. However, groups that have a less integral approach should also find the ideas helpful. The ideas have been used by myself or by the 'A' and 'B' Teams in Sheffield (see page 35). They can be used as described or adapted to meet the needs of your group, venue or teaching style. They are intended to spark off your own ideas and to be a springboard for developing a programme best suited to your group of children.

The book is divided into sections as follows:

PART ONE
Start Here

What better place to start? This part of the book will help you to set up your children's club. It looks at:

- why you should think of running one;
- what you should consider;
- equipment you might need;
- how to get going.

Also included is the 'Story of One Group' and 'More Approaches' to the way you might choose to organise your group. There are so many different ways that a children's club can be run that these are given for your consideration and to help you to choose the right way for you.

Finally, we look at how to use this book to plan a session.

PART TWO
This is where the ideas begin.

Activities for gathering together and setting the scene

The first three sections, which cover 'Icebreakers', 'Craft' and 'Food' can be used in this way. 'Bible links' and 'Using the idea' are given should you want to use the games and activities for 'setting the scene' but the ideas can be used in their own right for fun, team building, fair play and settling back into the group. A lot may have happened for the children since the last meeting so a 'gathering together time' helps them to get back into the group and the way it works.

Having fun together through games and challenges

Having fun together is an important aspect of any session. This, hopefully, will have happened in the opening activity and be continued through Sections 4, 5 and 6 with 'Energetic Games', 'Not-so-Energetic Games' and 'Party Games / Challenges'. 'Bible links' and 'Using the idea' are also given for those times when you may want to set the scene for your Bible time or go from your Bible time into a game but, again, these don't have to be used. Playing games is important for fun, using up energy, developing relationships with the leaders and the other children and team building.

Focusing together on Jesus

Finally, we look at different ways of 'Telling Stories' and 'Prayer and Praise'. These sections are intended to be more directly focused on talking to the children about Jesus and providing the opportunity for them to talk to God if they want to. They include games and activities that encourage children to be more receptive to the teaching and to release them into prayer and praise.

PART THREE

This includes useful resources, recipes and addresses. There is also an index of themes and an index of Bible references.

Enjoy the book, and let the ideas spark off ideas of your own. You know your children and what will work best with them. May this book be a springboard.

PART ONE

START HERE

Why children's clubs and when?
Before we answer these questions, we need to ask another:

What do you do on Sunday?

The children's answers might be …

- go to Dad's / Mum's;
- visit Grandma;
- go shopping / swimming / bowling;
- play outside;
- go out for the day.

And some of us might answer …

- go to church.

Today's children do not have quite the lifestyle we may have grown up with. Sundays have changed and we have to accept that going to church is not a priority for most families. Greater mobility has opened up new activities and even just visiting family members can take longer because people live further apart. We also have to ask if church is the best place to introduce children to Jesus if their families are not sharing in this with them.

If Sunday is not a good day for children to come to church, when is?
Groups on Saturdays and midweek are where we are seeing growth within the church's work among children at the moment. Why? Are these the better days for children to come and, if so, why are they better? The answers may be:

- Children are looking for something to do.
- Parents are happy for them to go somewhere for an hour while they go shopping or enjoy being without the children for a while.
- For some parents, perhaps, it salves their conscience, because deep down they feel their children should be receiving spiritual input.
- Groups midweek and on Saturdays do not interfere with family activities on Sundays.

This does not mean that we 'jump on the bandwagon' regardless, but it does mean that we may want to give thought and prayer as to whether this is the direction that God would have our church go.

So we come back to the question:

Why should we consider having a children's club?
Such groups are not new. Uniformed and other activity groups have been going on for years, and there seems to be a resurgence in popularity at present. Very few children now attend a traditional Sunday school and there is a special place for the group that provides the Christian teaching children are no longer receiving from school.

So, why should we consider running such a group in our church?

- Children are looking for something to do after school or on Saturdays.
- Some children are left to roam the streets and are grateful for somewhere to go.
- Some parents are too afraid to let their children go out by themselves but welcome an organised activity.
- Difficulties at home or school can make it hard for children to feel loved, develop a skill (eg music, dancing, swimming) or just succeed at something.
- The church is here to minister to the lost and to go out and meet people where they are.
- Simply to show love to the community.

Children's clubs can take many forms
For example, there is the 'first contact' group, which uses activities, games and songs to support basic teaching, and in which children from your church may also be involved. A first contact group can be a good place for children to bring their non-Christian friends.

Where to meet
Children's clubs are meeting in …

- churches or church halls;
- community centres;
- schools;
- private homes.

Ideas have been drawn from different approaches and venues with the objective of giving the reader confidence to try them and then to develop their own.

Shall we go for it?

What do we need to do before we make a decision? A good start is to pray. Praying is what makes a children's club run by Christians different from one run by non-Christians. It is important that not only we as the leaders of the club but also the church know what God wants us to do and who will do it. To find out, we need to ask him and to hear his answer. I remember asking God to show me whether I should lead an activity group for children under five. If I was to do this, I asked God to give me ideas for the programme for the next term. He did and I led the group. Later, when it came to a midweek group for non-church children, I did the same thing, but I not only asked him for the programme – I wanted a whole host of leaders too. I got enough to launch the group.

Pray on your own and with those who share your vision; pray for discernment for when it is right to start the club.

Seek support from the church. Others may have had a similar vision years before it was God's time to develop it and knowing this will be an encouragement to you and to the church. And prayer should continue as you plan the launch, the programme and week by week as the group establishes and develops.

Gaining the support of others

You will need the support of your church leadership – vicar, PCC, pastor, elders, minister, church meeting – whatever your church calls your leadership team. And you will need financial support. You should discuss this with the church leadership and ask the following questions: Will the money come from the church for initially setting up the club? Will the church be in regular support? Are grants available from other bodies?

You will need leaders and helpers. Check out the adult / child ratio which is given in your church's child protection guidelines. Think about the leadership gifts and skills necessary to run the group. Following is a list of some of the roles that will need to be filled. You may not need them all, but some are essential and some people may do more than one job.

- A leader with overall responsibility.
- Someone to handle registration / administration.
- Someone to organise publicity.
- A treasurer (if handling money).
- Someone to make squash, wash up and sort out messy activities.
- A team to prepare the venue.

- A first aider.
- Leaders who are able to lead specific activities like games, craft or storytelling.
- Someone able to provide musical accompaniment.

You may need to invite others from church with these skills to visit occasionally, and you might want to attend training courses to improve your own gifts and skills.

Also you will need people prepared to pray on a regular basis.

Some of the above don't need attendance at meetings and can involve the elderly or housebound. This can help them to feel valued and a part of the children's ministry. Some children's clubs take photographs of all the children and, with the children's and their parents' permission, give these to prayer partners who pray regularly for the children.

Getting ready to go

Having made the decision to start, you may want to ask the question: Who is the club for? Is it for:

- church kids;
- non-church kids;
- both together;
- mixed ages?

Where will the club meet?

You will need to consider the following:

- Venue – the church, church hall, community room, school, someone's home?
- How many will the venue hold?
- What type of activities can it be used for?
- Are there any obvious safety hazards that will influence your choice?
- Insurance – of building / children / leaders.
- Cost of hiring the venue.

When will the club meet?

You may want to consider these questions:

- What else is offered to children and when in your locality?

- Are other churches running a club on the same day that you have chosen? If so, should you change day or join forces with them?
- Does it have to be every week? Could it be once a month?

This challenges our thinking as to what's sensible for the children. Ideally, they need to be able to get into a routine to encourage attendance. The frequency also has to be within the capability of the leadership team, and to fit in with other things going on in the venue. Do you want to be crossing paths with other groups? Will the children be safe with others in the building?

For how long will the club meet?

An hour seems to be a reasonable length of time.

How much will it cost?

Consideration needs to be given to funding before you begin. Will the church fund it or is the group to be self-supporting? If the latter, what is a reasonable amount to ask children to pay? Do other groups in the town charge? If so, what? Ask around.

If a charge is to be made, think how this will be collected and recorded. A treasurer will be a useful member of the team – although not necessarily in attendance at meetings. The money can be collected in at registration. Some clubs that charge have a free 'come and see night' and then charge for the next meeting.

Will the children be divided into teams?

Having the children divided into teams will help with grouping and pastoral care. Children can work in these groups for craft, be together in team games, sit as a team for the story, join together for prayer, discussions and to drink squash, and share a time for news and getting to know one another. It can also help with discipline, as the group leader can address issues with the children individually or as a team. The children know who is responsible for them. If you choose to run a reward or points system, this can also be used to reinforce good behaviour.

Reward systems

Before you launch, you may want to consider whether or not to run an individual or group reward system. Reward systems can be effective but they also come with a 'health warning'! There are advantages and disadvantages. Some groups have used them effectively for years and other groups have not found them to be so helpful, so let's look at the advantages and disadvantages of such a system.

Advantages: The advantages of a reward system are that it can assist discipline, encourage attendance and, if children are in teams, encourage team building, with children behaving so as not to let their team down.

Disadvantages: The disadvantages are administrating it (if it's not your thing); too much competition could make some children feel a failure; it can damage self-esteem; and it can encourage bullying.

If you decide to use a reward system, here's how it can work. Points can be awarded for:

- attendance;
- behaviour;
- bringing a friend;
- learning the memory verse;
- sitting quietly for story;
- helpfulness.

Rewards can be given as points, punches in a card, stickers on a card or coloured square on a card. These points can be collected by individuals or by the team leader.

At the end of a given time, either weekly, monthly or half-termly, the children are presented with individual or group prizes or certificates.

Prizes such as pens, notepads or keyrings could have texts printed on them. If going to the highest scoring boy and girl over a longer period of time, the prize could be something bigger like a Christian book.

The competitive element can be minimised by making it more an individual reward system. Some groups have the children collect points which can be exchanged in the tuck shop, leaving children to decide when they use them. The points add up to a certain value for exchange so the children can aim high, if they wish – books come at the 'higher point' range. Research shows that you have to change the rewards to maintain the effectiveness of the system. Introducing choice may assist the effectiveness of the system.

Another way of using the reward system idea is to run one short-term for a specific project or if there is a behaviour or other problem in the group.

Some thoughts on discipline

All the children will feel more secure if they know that they are safe and that others will not be able to hurt them in any way. It is therefore important to address discipline problems as soon as they arise. So, what do you do if one or more children are badly behaved? If the programme is action packed and fast moving, this question may not arise, but even in the best led groups some children may not behave very well for a number of reasons which may have nothing to do with the club. Some children have problems at home or school that they bring in with them. These may include having a reputation at school to live up to, and being bullied or being a bully.

Should a problem arise, try to have a leader close by – for instance, if they are messing around in a 'Together time', have a leader sit with them.

If you are using a reward system, let it work for you; give points for good or improved behaviour. And talk to the children involved. Find out why they are behaving like this. Do they want to be noticed? Do they not want to come to the club?

The children need to know that they have a choice. They do not have to come to the club – it is not like school – but if they do come, spoiling the time for other children is not acceptable. The leaders also have a choice. They can choose to say that if it is in the best interest of the other children in the club, a particular child or group of children can be asked not to come for a week. Parents can be told why. This may seem a bit radical but it also sets a framework and provides boundaries for the children. If the children concerned want to come, they will at least try to be more co-operative next time. If they only want to be disruptive, they need to know that this won't be allowed.

Decisions like this can involve the other children in the group. We had to say 'no' to a group of children and, after one week when they came again, the other children wanted us to give them another chance to show that they could behave. Interestingly, the children who regularly came to the club also saw it as the Christian thing to do – a bit like 'What Would Jesus Do?' The children being disruptive were also new to the group and the other children suggested that it may be that they were finding it difficult to fit in. They didn't yet know how the club worked and so they could be covering embarrassment by being disruptive.

Their argument was, 'Now they know, they need a second chance.' We gave them one and saw improvement.

You may choose to visit the child at home and talk with the parents or to take advice from school teachers in your church.

Caring for the leaders

It is important that the leaders are cared for and that they have the support and training they need. For this you will need regularly to review your workload and that of your team and to make sure you and they are not over-stretched.

Look at the skills you and your helpers have. How can these be developed? Would it help to have mentors from in or outside the church?

Your church leadership / group management team need to ensure that you have the care and support that you need.

Developing skills

The gifts, skills, abilities and expertise of your team need to be recognised and appreciated. There may be areas of training that individual leaders would like to undertake or that the whole leadership team could attend together. Training courses are offered by national organisations like Children's Ministry, Church Pastoral Aid Society, Scripture Union and various denominational bodies.

- Find out if your church has a training budget. Giving financial support can encourage your leaders to attend conferences and training days.
- Ask your leaders if there is a particular area of training that they would like and help to make this happen for them.
- Encourage attendance at team meetings and team training, which can be given 'in house'. 'Child protection' awareness training is now becoming a must in most churches.

Pastoral care / mentors

All of us need support and someone to talk to and bounce ideas off, especially when the going gets tough. It is good to have thought about this beforehand and for your leaders to know who they will look to for this support. It may be that they will look to the group leader and certainly the leaders will look to each other to plan, debrief and review each session. However, you may want more than that.

Pastoral care for the leaders may be in the form of mentors. Mentoring is not new but the terminology has not been in use in most of our churches. Many

Christians have prayer partners, some have spiritual advisers, others spiritual directors. Pastoral care may be given by housegroup or cell leaders, and the vicar, minister or pastor can provide this too. These people can also fulfil a mentoring role – someone available to support, encourage and challenge. Another name for a mentor is a 'coach', so even though you may have pastoral care, a prayer partner, spiritual adviser or spiritual director in place, you may want someone with experience in children's ministry to act as a 'coach' for you. However, your mentor does not necessarily have to have experience in working with children to be effective for you.

One of the prime functions of a mentor is to listen to you and to pray with you. In listening, the mentor can bring an outside perspective on your whole life and not just the ministry side of it; we all need balance. It is easy to be overstretched or overwhelmed and your mentor can help you to keep things in perspective and address any problems. They also encourage and support.

So what are the characteristics of a mentor? They should be:

- a good listener;
- objective;
- able to give honest feedback in a positive way;
- able to give care, encouragement and support.

Some ground rules and expectations need to be set. Here are some to think about:

- How often will you meet?
- The mentor needs to know the areas in your life that you are wanting to look at – does he or she have a responsibility to stretch you or just support you?
- Openness of discussion – do you want the bad news as well as the good?
- How will you ensure confidentiality?
- How long will this relationship last?

Caring for the children – Child Protection

Your church should have a child protection policy. If you are not already familiar with it, ask to see a copy. This is essential reading. If your church does not have such a policy, ask the church leadership to produce one for you. They can take advice from their denominational Children's Officer, who should have developed agreed guidelines for their churches; or take advice from the Churches' Child Protection Advisory Service.

The Churches Child Protection Advisory Service (CCPAS) is an independent Christian-based charity that provides training, resources, advice and support in all areas of child protection and good working practice, as well as a 24-hour helpline.

Resources include *'Guidance to Churches'*, a fully comprehensive child protection manual incorporating model policies on child protection and safe practice that can be downloaded from the accompanying CD. As well as conducting live *'Facing the Unthinkable'* child protection training seminars, a complete DVD distance learning training pack of the same name is also available.

As an umbrella body appointed by the Criminal Records Bureau, CCPAS is able to process criminal records checks quickly and efficiently. Its work is endorsed by the Department of Health and the Department for Education and Skills.

Make sure that the following guidelines are observed:

- All leaders and helpers should have filled in the appropriate forms and signed the confidential declarations.
- References should be taken up.
- The leaders and helpers should be accepted and appointed by your church council.
- All leaders and helpers should have a job description and thus know what is expected of them.
- All leaders and helpers should attend child protection training as required by your church. (This training is as much for the protection of the leaders as it is for the children.)
- All leaders and helpers should know to whom they are accountable.
- All leaders and helpers should be provided with pastoral care.

Your child protection policy will also give you the following:

- A safe adult-to-child ratio.
- Application forms for parents to complete before their children attend the group.

- Off-site activity forms.
- Procedure to prevent child abuse within the group – including bullying.
- Procedure for if you suspect a child is abused – within the group or elsewhere.
- Suggested contents of your first aid box.
- Advice on the transport of children.

Following your child protection guidelines not only protects the children but also protects the leaders. It creates a safer environment for everyone.

Fire regulations

We don't plan to have fires in our clubs but we have to be prepared and to know what we will do should this happen. So what should we do?

- Know where the fire exits are and check that they are clearly marked.
- Know where the fire fighting appliances and fire blankets are and how to use them.
- Leaders need to know of their responsibilities:
  - Who will escort children from the building?
  - Who will take action over the fire, use the fire extinguisher or fire blanket and, if necessary, ring the fire brigade?
  - Who will have the register of children and adults present in the building?
  - Where will the children assemble?
- Children need to be told, and a fire drill held, so that they know what to do.

Launch ... ready to go

The launch is important and you will want to let as many people as possible know about your new group. The key to this is good publicity. It is essential to advertise the group if you want children from the community to come. This can be done in various ways:

- Invitations through church children to friends, direct to schools, or through your local library.
- Big splash through local newspaper – something to catch attention and interest, like a big silly event, eg largest banana split in the county, or a community art wall.
- Holiday club – this can be led by your children's club leadership team with

the advantage that the children will see the same leaders at the end of the holiday club. Or you could invite someone in with experience in such events – though that may be difficult to follow.

We had to face this one when we had a holiday club as part of a church mission led by a gifted children's evangelist who was a ventriloquist. How could we follow that? But we did follow it, and soon had our own puppets whispering in our ears!

The invitation

This needs to be as eye-catching, visual and colourful as you can make it. You want the children to like what they see and, as a result, to want to come.

You may want to include:

- name of group;
- name of church running it;
- where (venue);
- when (day and starting date);
- time;
- age range;
- cost, if any;
- kind of activities, eg craft / games / story / puppets / parachute / etc, that you will be doing.

Useful equipment

Most clubs are run on a low budget, but if you are given money to set up, or can raise money, it can be a good investment to buy larger pieces of equipment like a parachute, puppets, flags or, if you are planning to play a lot of team games, suitable sports equipment.

Parachutes

We have found a play parachute to be an invaluable piece of equipment. Parachutes can be bought cheaply from your local Army and Navy Store but, if you can afford a more expensive one specially made for play it will respond better to the activities you will be using it for and it is more colourful. One supplier is SeamStress Ltd. Some ideas for different uses for parachutes will be found later in this book.

If you cannot buy your own parachute, you may be able to borrow one for special occasions from your diocesan, denominational, or local authority resource centre. For some activities, large muslin sheets or a king-size bed sheet can be substituted.

Puppets

Puppets are another large expense but again if you plan to use them regularly, they are a good investment. It may be that a children's puppet ministry team could develop out of your group. Details for setting up a puppet ministry and for training courses can be obtained from One Way UK.

Puppets are invaluable for storytelling, story review, leading singing, group identification. They can be muppet style, large 'Sooty' style or marionettes. They can be people or animals. The muppet style is particularly impressive and these are the ones most used in puppet ministry.

Other puppets are just as effective. We used a large Disney/Pixar character to sit in the crook of my arm and whisper in my ear. One of the younger children was convinced that he was talking to me and asked if he might whisper in her ear too!

Flags and ribbons

Flags and ribbons can add variety to worship. Teaching the children how to use them, and working out movements with them to the words of songs, can help to reinforce teaching as the children fit expressive action to words and music with the flag or ribbon. Working together in a small group or as a large group can give a feeling of 'belonging' and achievement as they participate.

Flags and ribbons can be made (see Part Three) or purchased from suppliers like Kingdom Dance Resources Limited, who also have available booklets of choreographed dances and can offer training courses, as can the Christian Dance Fellowship of Britain.

Sports equipment

Your choice of equipment will depend upon your building facility. If you have a sports hall you may want football goal nets, basketball rings, etc. Even without these facilities, you may want to have foldaway goal nets or movable basketball posts. These can be obtained from shops like The Early Learning Centre.

Additional equipment

For games:

- soft indoor balls
- hoops
- bean bags
- containers (we use buckets)

For craft

- tables
- paint
- paintbrushes
- glue
- glue spreaders
- glue sticks
- felt pens
- pencils
- paper
- card
- scissors

Music

This needs to have street cred with the children. We have used CDs by Doug Horley, Jim Bailey and Shane Roots with non-church children. They particularly like music that sounds like the music they listen to at home. We have also used songs by Ishmael, Alan Price, John Hardwick and Ralph Ward. With all music you will need to listen to the tracks and select what appeals to your children and what will achieve your objective. Ask children you know what they like. This doesn't rule out 'older' songs which can still have their place, and songs the children sing in school will give familiarity.

You will need either your own musicians, or a good tape or CD player and a collection of suitable tapes and CDs for the children to sing along to.

If you are using pre-recorded music, you will need to have a Performing Rights Society church licence and, maybe, a Phonographic Performance Licence. Details can be obtained from Christian Copyright Licensing International. If you are projecting songs onto acetates, you will need to check whether your church has a Church Copyright Licence and, if you wish to photocopy music, your church will need a Music Reproduction Licence as well. (These are also available from Christian Copyright Licensing.) Check with your church first as many churches already hold these licences if they reproduce songs or music in any form. Your church's copyright administrator will ask you to keep a list of the songs you are using and the music you are photocopying so that these can be recorded on the sheets that they are required to return to CCLI each year.

We have lift off!

You have prayed and prepared. You have attended the training courses that you need to attend – and there will be plenty more that you can attend as time goes by. You have read the books that you need to read – and there are more of those too. And now you are ready to 'go for it'!

You may be aware of your limitations but you believe that God is calling you to run this children's club so go for it in the knowledge that 'those he calls he equips'.

You may want to ask the church leadership team to commission you and pray over you.

First meeting

You will need a plan for the meeting. One suggestion is:

- registration
- opening activity
- a game
- song
- story
- squash
- review teaching
- prayer

This pattern worked for us. See also 'The Story of One Group' and 'More Approaches' for other ideas.

In more detail

Decide on the theme for your meeting. We chose to have the name of our group as the theme. So our first meeting went like this:

- Theme – name of group: BUGZ (Building Up God's Zone).

- Registration and grouping children into teams.
- Opening activity (7 minutes) – make bugs using coloured modelling clay in teams.
- Parachute games (15 minutes).
- Sing (5 minutes) – we sang 'Jesus' love is very wonderful' because the children had been singing it in the holiday club.
- Introduce Group Puppet and the name of the club (5 minutes).
- Squash and biscuits and group time in teams (10 minutes).
- Story (10 minutes) – 'Bugs in the Bible', the story of Moses and Pharaoh in Exodus 8.
- Sing (5 minutes) – 'Prayer is like a mobile phone' (favourite from the holiday club).
- Pray (3 minutes).
- Home time – taking bugs, made in opening activity, home in a bag.

Over the weeks that followed, we introduced mascots for each team using the resources available through Disney/Pixar from the *Bug's Life* range so our teams were named Ants, Caterpillars, Beetles and Fleas. The group mascot was the *Bug's Life* character, Flik. We named him BUGZ, after the group name, and the children quickly accepted this.

Keeping in touch

It is important to keep in touch with the children, especially if they miss a week or two. Some leaders like to make weekly home visits and this can be fruitful if you and your leaders have the time and the families welcome you. Then if a child does miss a week, it gives you the opportunity to find out why they were not present and gives the children and their parents the message that the church cares about them. It reflects the love of Jesus and builds up relationships with families.

If you cannot visit in person a card could be sent or a telephone call made.

Impact of follow up

The value of keeping in touch cannot be overestimated. All of us need to know that others care about us and a visit, card or telephone call will reflect the love of Jesus to the children.

This is borne out in our locality by a youth worker who rings his youth group members every week, with the result that they look forward to the next youth meeting. It's hard for them to resist a personal invitation, especially when it's to be with a selected group of young people.

Reaching parents

Although we want to see whole families come to faith, our main aim in keeping in contact with parents should be one of care and interest, for this will break down suspicion and fear. In time, they may ask questions about our faith or ask to come on an Alpha course. The 323 Club mentioned in 'More Approaches' serves coffee and also runs an Alpha course during the club's session time as a means of reaching parents. Getting to know parents and allowing them to get to know us – or other members of the church as coffee is served – could be the bridge that helps them to come to faith.

Building bridges develops trust between parents and the children's group leaders. This can help the children to feel more secure and be better behaved, because they know that we are in touch with their parents. It also helps to break down barriers of suspicion or fear and parents or carers will feel secure with us, and be more likely to ask questions about our faith. This will present the opportunity to answer their questions and, in time, to invite them to an Alpha or similar course. One father in our church so appreciated the support given during a difficult time in his family, and for his daughter at school, that he asked if he could attend an Alpha course.

So how do we build bridges?

Social activities

Most of us have busy schedules and we are not looking for more work, so let's look at what's already happening in our church social calendar and see if we can invite our children's families to join in. For this we will need to talk to the organisers of each event and, if it's a suitable activity, ask them if we can invite our non-church parents or carers.

Suitable activities might be …

- skittles night
- walk
- treasure hunt
- barbecue

- sports afternoon
- video
- meal

Invitations to your club meetings

Parents may be reluctant to come to church, but may not mind joining in the last few minutes of the club meeting. Suitable times would be Christmas for carol singing and mince pies, Mothering Sunday (but does this have to be on Sunday?) and Easter or Harvest.

When do you invite parents to church?

Parents are more likely to come to church if their children are taking part in the service and if they know other people who will be there. So you could try the following:

- Plan a children's club service.
- Invite parents or carers to an all-age service.
- Have children take part in the service.
- Send out invitations ahead of time – the children can make these.
- Make sure that someone they recognise from the children's club is part of the welcoming team – they need to see a friendly face.
- Serve tea and coffee with the children handing round biscuits.

It's worth it

Showing love to the community costs us in terms of time and commitment, not just for the meeting time but for preparation, prayer and follow-up, but it is worth it to see results like these:

- Regular attendance (most of the time!).
- Children 'owning' the group.
- The change in the children. (For some this is the one place where they feel valued.)
- The building up of trust.
- Friendship with families.
- Fun, laughter, friends and learning about Jesus.
- Children growing in relationship with the leaders and with other children.
- Children getting to know Jesus.

THE STORY OF ONE GROUP

This is the story of one group meeting, rather unusually, in a home on a council estate in Sheffield. The children are divided into teams according to age, with the 'A' team for the 4–7s, the 'B' team for the 8–11s and the 'C' team for the 12–15s. This group began in 1989 with eleven 8–11 year old children. All the groups used to meet in the same house but the 'C' team now meet elsewhere. The 'A' and 'B' teams meet on the same night and follow a similar programme. Each group meets for one hour and current attendance is twenty children in the 'A' team and thirty-nine in the 'B' team.

There is no church on the estate and the leaders have found that whereas parents would not let their children go to a church, they would let them go to someone's home. All the parents know that this is a Christian group. They are given a copy of the aims of the group when they register their children. Interestingly, they relate to the leader in the same way that they might to the church pastor or minister, and because she is one of their neighbours they readily pop in to discuss their problems or to seek help over a cup of tea for things like filling in forms.

A typical evening

Before the meeting starts, one of the leaders is always on 'door duty' to make sure there are no undesirables around and that the children arrive safely. Shoes are left in the hall, coats are put in two piles in the kitchen – girls and boys.

On arrival the children go into the kitchen to have a hole punched in their card for attending and one extra hole if they went to church on Sunday. Any new details are taken and the register is marked. The children then go into the lounge and join in with the opening activity, often a game. This is the beginning of a fast-moving programme – which is needed to keep the children's attention.

The programme is similar to that of groups meeting in more traditional venues. The evening begins with the 'A' team.

6pm: Opening game, party style, eg pass the parcel, hunt the thimble, musical bumps. Children join in as they arrive.

6.10: News and prayer time. An object is passed round the group and the children who want to share their news do so when they are holding the object. If they don't want to say anything, they pass the object to the next child. The leaders listen out for items for prayer, eg new shoes, baby ill, Grandma's died, Dad's left home. The children join in the praying. To help the flow, those who want to pray line up and they pray down the line.

6.20: Story using flannelgraph, overhead slides, drama, etc. This is usually a Bible story but sometimes a secular story is used to get a Christian message over, eg about bullying, stealing, cheating. Sometimes this is followed up in small groups and can lead to prayer.

6.35: Orange squash and biscuits are served in the kitchen.

6.40: Library time. The children can borrow a book from the two hundred or so Christian books laid out by two of the young helpers on the twin beds in a bedroom upstairs. The library is very well used and parents also borrow a book sometimes – if there is nothing much to watch on the television!

6.45: Worship time, using the overhead projector and at least one guitar and, occasionally, percussion instruments. During this time, the children can go to the kitchen for prayer if they want to.

6.55: Prayers and prizes. A final prayer is said, stickers are added up and one prize given (see below).

6.59: Coats are brought in. Shoes have been taken to the kitchen after the drinks have been cleared away. While this is happening, the 'B' team are arriving. They leave their shoes in the hall, take their coats with them into the lounge until the 'A' team have left and then it all starts again.

At the end, a leader watches the children from the gate as they leave while other leaders supervise their leaving from the house.

Reward system

This group uses a reward system. When a child has twenty-five punches (fifty after the first twenty-five) they receive a small prize of a key ring, biro or pencil, each with a text on. Children are also given stickers through the evening for winning games, good behaviour, answering questions, etc.

Special occasions

At Christmas, they have 150 parents and children squashed into the lounge over-spilling into the hall and up the stairs. Special guests of national renown attend with delight, interest and amazement. The children enact the nativity.

At Easter, another invitation is issued to parents (remember this is an average size council house!). The leader's motto is 'Furniture out to get people in'. Each week, all her furniture and ornaments are moved out of the room and then returned when the last children have gone. For special occasions, even the doors are taken off their hinges to get everyone in. Equipment for the evenings is stored in an outhouse.

Sports Day is the finale of the year. This is held on a field at the back of the house with 200 people attending. They have races, a God spot and a special guest.

Not many of us will be called of God to use our homes in this way but what a story! It shows what can be done in even the simplest setting.

MORE APPROACHES

There are many ways of organising your session and you must choose one that is right for you. The following are included as ideas only. They may help you to shape your thinking. The time of day, the venue, the kind of children you aim to reach, the message you want to give, the length of meeting, the age range of children – all these will influence how you choose to run the group. We begin with an after-school club, working in partnership with a school at the school's request.

1. 'The Blitz' after-school club

The Blitz meets after school once a week between 3.30pm and 5pm. This group charges 30p to attend and meets in the church. It is aimed at children aged from 9–12 (school Years 5,6 and 7) and has as its Mission Statement 'Make friends and make Jesus known'.

A sample programme

3pm: Leaders set up room and pray together.

3.30: Children arrive and register. They are offered a drink and something to eat, usually a packet of crisps, doughnut or chocolate biscuit.
The children then have a choice of activity, eg:

- Games – Twister, Connect 4, Boppit Extreme, Table Football, etc.
- Football or cricket outside if weather permits.
- Play Station.
- Craft – Hammer bead boards, finger painting, using Polaroid cameras to make passports.
- Cooking – cakes, pizzas, toasted sandwiches, etc. This is only offered once every two to three weeks.
- Video – Disney style.

4.25: Group activity – parachute, hockey, games.

4.45: Talk which may include gospel story using illusions, dramatisation, etc.

4.58: Notices.

5.00: Home time.

2. The 323 Club

The 323 Club meets between 6.30pm and 8pm one day a week in the church and is aimed at children aged from 4 to 10. It costs 10p to attend and its Mission

Statement is 'To give kids and leaders the best one-and-a-half hours of their week, and to have God at the heart'.

The club is in a tough area of the town. As well as reaching the children, the church is also concerned to reach out and give support to the parents. They do this by serving coffee and chatting to parents during the session and they have now started an Alpha course for interested parents during that time.

A sample programme

6.10: Staff meeting and prayer.

6.30: Doors open. The children arrive and are registered. They are then offered something to eat from the tuck shop. Children then choose from:

- games set up
- football outside (in suitable weather)
- craft activity
- cooking

7.10: Groups: children gather with their group leader for an activity related to the theme for the evening.

7.35: Up front time (led from the front)

- songs
- story or talk
- quiz

8.00: Drink and home time.

3. Kids Quest

Kids Quest meets in the church weekly for an hour during term time. It runs with two alternating leadership teams which meet together before each term to decide on that term's theme. The leadership teams keep in touch to ensure a varied programme. For example, if one team has concentrated on games one week, the other will concentrate on videos or stories the next. They aim to provide a balanced, exciting and varied programme.

Children are given individual points for attending, taking part in games, crafts and quizzes and for being part of the winning group in team games. These points are exchanged for gifts at the end of the term. The children are only split into teams for the purpose of games and then only on a random basis.

Kids Quest has a board within the church for displaying work so a craft activity is planned as an ongoing weekly project.

A sample programme

6pm: As the children arrive they do something on the ongoing weekly project for the display board in church.

6.10: Active game.

6.20: Story, quiz, video or special guest.

6.35: Activity time. (For example, they have made gifts, cards, banana splits, toffee apples and performed plays.)

6.45: Buffer time. (Something is held in reserve in case it is needed.)

6.50: Crisps and drinks. Place display items on board. Talk to children about next week and anything they might need to bring.

7pm: Home time.

This group also visits a local residential home for the elderly.

Some themes for their display board have been:

- 'Fruit of the Spirit.' A mosaic in the shape of a basket was placed on the board with children adding a different fruit to the mosaic each week.
- Easter. Three crosses with the words
  – rejection – one thief
  – acceptance – other thief
  – forgiveness – Christ
- The body. A life-size outline was put up on the board. Christ was the head. Each week different parts of the body (arms, hands, legs) were added.

4. Workshop choices

Another way of organising your session time is to have workshop choices. After the initial opening activities, the children can choose between the workshops on offer and, depending on the workshops and how long you think you will need for them, maybe half of your meeting time will be devoted to these. This enables a longer activity to be included in the programme from time to time.

Workshop ideas:

- tie-dyeing
- pottery
- ceramic or wood painting
- baking

- drama and dance
- football or basketball training

5. Soccer club (Mini-Soccer 4–4–2)

A first-contact group can also take the form of a soccer (or other sports) club or a craft, dance or drama club. The Mission Statement for these clubs may be 'Being Jesus in the world'. Although such groups are not the focus of this book, they can play a valuable role in making contact with youngsters in the community, building up relationships and developing trust. Christian values will be seen in action through fair play and by the way we treat the youngsters and allow them to treat each other.

Our church runs Mini-Soccer 4–4–2 on a Saturday morning. This was set up for church and non-church youngsters in the 9–16 age range – most attending are non-church. They play in inter-church league matches. Slowly, as these youngsters make friends with each other and with the leaders, they will venture into the bar (non-alcoholic) that we have in the church. This is another step towards finding out about Jesus. Play Stations, table games and a pool table are set up in the bar and youth friendly music is played. They meet other youngsters at the bar who are Christians and there are Christian adults around. The more they are identifying with the soccer club and the bar, the more receptive they are to invitations to street-cred DJ style youth services and, further down the track, wanting to find out about Jesus for themselves.

USING THIS BOOK TO PLAN A SESSION

Having decided on the plan for the evening and chosen a theme, how do you use this book to put together the programme? The book is divided into sections from which you can make your choices. You will need a gathering activity to begin with to set the scene – an icebreaker, craft or food activity.

In making your choice for this, you will need to think about the number of leaders you have available at this time. Some will be registering children. Others may be watching the approach to your venue, welcoming the children and their parents to the group. Others may still be sorting out the drinks – unless you are really well organised and ahead of time. The ideal of course is to have everything ready, with the leaders arriving early enough to do this and have time to pray together before the session begins but, from my experience, this doesn't always work out!

After the gathering activity, you will want to plan a varied and fast-moving programme which could include games, story, craft, news time, group time, prayer, etc. The story may be told through a game or a craft activity; prayer time may be similar or an extension of talking to each other leading on to talking to God. There are many different approaches so feel free to put together a programme that suits you. There is no set way.

To begin to plan your programme you will need a notebook and pen. Then I suggest that you pray. Ask God for a theme for the session – or even for the half term. The example given below uses the theme of the Prodigal Son (Luke 15), starts at 6pm and lasts for one hour. Your group may be at a different time and last for longer than an hour; the time and activity choices can be adapted accordingly.

6pm Register and opening activity in groups

Look in the Subject Index of this book under Prodigal Son or under Pigs. For example, you could choose to make marshmallow pigs (idea 27). Or you could play a circle game using pigs as described in idea 53. Jot down your choices.

6.10 Game

Look in the games sections and choose a game. The game does not have to link to the theme but if you want it to, and if there's not a suitable linked suggestion, choose one of the games and adapt it. For example, you could choose the Relay Race, idea 40, and adopt it as follows:

- Mark team line with masking tape.
- Have food for the 'pigs' at one end of the room (eg bean bags, small balls) in a bowl or bucket.
- Children stand in a line. On command 'Go' the first child runs to the bowl or bucket, takes out one bit of 'food', carries it back, crosses the team line and places the food in the home bucket.
- The next player sets off as player in front crosses the team line. This continues until all the children have had their turn or, if teams are not equal, all the food is in the home bucket. Some children may have to run twice.
- The winning team is the first to be sitting down with the front child holding the bucket with all the food in it.

6.25 Song

A song that the group knows could be chosen. For widening the children's repertoire of songs, look at CDs in a Christian bookshop and choose one that you like. Suggestions are given in the Resources section.

For this theme, one possibility is *'Nobody's a nobody'* by John Hardwick (© 1993 Daybreak Music) from the tape *I'm No Cartoon* (PIP Productions). Or you might choose *'The Lord loves me'* from Ishmael's *Songs for Little Children* (Ishmael © 1999 Thankyou Music). Or *'Whoopah Wahey'*, from the CD of that name by Doug Horley (© 1999 Thankyou Music). These last 2 are available from Children's Ministry.

6.30 Story

Again, look in the Subject Index under Pigs. You may choose the story outlined in idea 27 or select your approach from the *Telling Stories* section of the book. One idea might be to take the dramatised story described in idea 70 and write your own in a similar way.

Possible words could be: Father, Son, Pigs, Friends. Suggested actions:
Father: stand up, arms out.
Son: stand up, walk on spot.
Pigs: on all fours, make piggy sounds.
Friends: stand, rub hands together, say 'chink, chink'.

As suggested in idea 70, divide the children into groups, or use the teams they are already in, and give each group a word to listen out for. Then tell your story.

6.35 Squash and group time

You will need to think about whether you will be serving drinks and, if so, when, how and where and whether you will be doing anything else during this time. This programme places drinks near the middle of the session and chooses to serve them to the children sitting in groups with their group leaders. You may want an older child to collect drinks and bring them to the group or you may prefer that an adult carries them over. The squash could be served from a jug or already be poured into the cups. Biscuits can also be served if you choose. We have found in our group (in an urban priority area) that some children do not have biscuits at home and having them at the club is a treat. The time can also be used for talking together.

After drinks, you will need to gather the children together again. We use the beginning of a lively song as a 'gathering call'. When the children hear the music play they rush to the 'gather spot' for the next activity. The first group ready wins the point.

When gathered together, what will you do? You might choose to sing another song.

6.45 Story review

You don't need to review the story but, if you choose to, this is one way of doing it. It is based on idea 74 which uses puppets. This can be played with or without a mascot, and can be done in a light-hearted way.

True or false quiz

1. ***With a mascot.*** You will need puppets as group mascots, and hoops.
   The children, on their turn, take the group mascot and stand in the hoop if the statement is true or on a line made of masking tape if it is false.

2. ***Without a mascot.***
   - Children stand in the middle of the room.
   - Name the walls on either side True and False.
   - Children make their choice of answer and run to the appropriate wall.

3. ***Questions.***
   - Ask the question (see idea 74 for examples).
   - Wait for the children to respond.
   - Give the right answer – True or False.

For other ideas look in the Subject Index under Story Review.

6.55 Closing prayer

It is good to close the meeting in some formal way so that everyone knows that it has finished. This example suggests a closing prayer. This could be said by one of the leaders or read out by a child. (See idea 93.)

7.00 Home

Your planning is nearly done. Look back over the notes you have made and select the ideas that seem the best for your group. Write out your final programme and any prompts to help you to remember what to do, eg for a game, the story, an activity, the prayer time. Plan to debrief afterwards with other leaders. What went well? What didn't? How were the children? How did the leaders feel about the session? This will help in planning the next session.

PART TWO

Section One:
Icebreakers

Some children will be queuing up outside long before you are ready to let them in and others will arrive a few minutes late, so an opening activity will enable the children to have something to do on arrival. This can be a whole group activity or, if your children are organised into teams, a team activity. Points can be awarded if this is part of your club organisation.

The opening activity can set the scene for the rest of the session or it can be a fun activity with no particular application to the teaching but which will develop relationships within the larger group or, where the children are divided into smaller groups, build up team identity. It may also be a craft or food activity (see Sections Two and Three) or a game (see Sections Four and Five).

'**Bible links**' and '**Using the idea**' are included should you wish to use the opening activity to set the scene for your teaching time.

Space Flight

This is a fun, active and easy-to-join-in game.

What you need: A space big enough for the activity.

What you do:

- The leader tells the children what to do for each manoeuvre of the space flight. Sound effects are optional!
  - Take off: jump up and down.
  - Land: crouch on the floor.
  - Boost: face a different way.
  - Dock: join up with someone else (suggest by linking arms).
  - Separate: let go of partner.
  - Orbit: rotate round your partner without touching them (face to face or back to back).

- Practise the movements and then play the game.
- The leader calls out the name of a manoeuvre and the children carry out the movement they have practised.
- Children join in as they arrive and when everyone is there it can be played competitively.
- The object then is to catch the children out. When out, these children can help watch the others.
- Winners are those still left at the end of the time set for the activity.
- Award points to the winners, or to their teams if you have team points.

Bible link

The Ascension (Acts 1:9–11).

Using the idea

After playing the game, tell the story of Jesus being taken up to heaven. He didn't go in quite the same way as space men go into space but 'he was taken up before their very eyes, and a cloud hid him from their sight' (Acts 1:9). Just as we would watch intently as a space rocket lifts off or as an aeroplane takes off, so Jesus' friends (disciples) watched. You may want to stop here or continue to tell the story of the two men dressed in white (angels) who told the disciples that Jesus 'will come back in the same way you have seen him go into heaven'.

ADDITIONAL IDEAS

1. Animals

- Kangaroos: jump.
- Rabbits: bunny jump.
- Elephants: raise trunk (lift arm up from nose).
- Fish: swim (hands together, fingers facing forward, move them in a wavy fashion).
- Birds: fly (flap arms).

Bible link

Creation (Genesis 1); the animals in the Ark (Genesis 6–8); Daniel's lions (Daniel 6).

Using the idea

Play the game and then tell the children your chosen story. See also ideas 12–14 (where the children create their own animals from play dough, clay or modelling clay, or provide cutters to make animals, sun, moon and stars from the play dough). Idea 15 suggests using animal masks – choose one animal from the activity above, or introduce one to fit the story and, having made a mask for that animal, tell the story of, for example, Daniel and the lions. See idea 54 for the story and the game 'Lions' stalk'. Alternatively see idea 35 for recipes for making animal-shaped biscuits.

2. Fireworks

Particularly good in November but can be used at other times of the year.

- Rockets: hands over head.
- Roman candles: arms up and down.
- Catherine wheels: circle one hand round and round in front of body.
- Bangers: lie on floor covering ears.

Bible link

Ezekiel 1:4 which talks about 'flashing lightning' and 'brilliant light'; the Transfiguration (Luke 9:28–36); Elijah's bonfire (1 Kings 18:16–46).

Using the idea

The Ezekiel passage is about the glory of God. This game could be used to think about the most beautiful firework display and so really enter into Ezekiel's vision. The story may help to answer the question, 'What does God look like?' Moses asked to see God's glory, but he was told that no one can see the face of God and live. He was allowed to see God's back (Exodus 33:18–23).

The Transfiguration is another passage dealing with the glory of the Lord.

After the game has been played, talk about fireworks that the children have seen. Let them tell you about their favourites and then ask them what else comes with fireworks. The answer you are looking for is 'a bonfire', which will lead you into the story of Elijah's bonfire in 1 Kings 18.

In the river, on the bank

This is a fast-moving, listening game.

What you need: Masking tape running down length of room.

What you do:

- Explain that one side of the tape is the river and the other side is the bank and show the children which is which.
- On the command 'In the river' or 'On the bank' the children jump over the tape to the side called.
- Have a few practice runs.
- This can be speeded up to help catch the children out.
- When all the children are familiar with the game, it can become a competition. The children on the wrong side of the tape are 'out'.
- When 'out' they cheer the others on.

- If you are using a reward system, this can be played as a team game with the winner scoring points for their team as well as for themselves.

Bible link

Crossing the Red Sea (Exodus 14); crossing of the Jordan (Joshua 3); Jesus' baptism (Luke 3:21–22).

Using the idea

After the game, tell the children your chosen Bible story. This could be read or enacted dramatically, using the marked out 'river bank'. You will need to add another line of masking tape to indicate both banks of the river (or sea).

1. Red Sea or the River Jordan

Talk to the children about the river bed. When the river parted for the people to cross, how easy was it to walk across? Was it flat or were there boulders in it? What size were the boulders? Could the people step over them or did they need to walk round them? How easy was it for them? See also idea 81.

There is an excellent illustration of this in the video Prince of Egypt (© Dream Works International LLC). If your church has a Performing Rights Licence to show videos (see page 30) an extract from this video could be shown. See also idea 79 for dramatising the story.

You may also want the children to think about how they might have felt. Develop this in small groups and encourage them to explore their own feelings about adventurous or unknown activities.

2. Jesus' baptism

Invite some volunteers to play the part of John and the people waiting to be baptised. As they enter the 'water' they kneel down and John pretends to pour water over them. Everyone else is the crowd on the bank.

Then Jesus comes and 'the crowd' become the witnesses of Jesus meeting John and asking John to baptise him. This can be mimed as you tell the story.

Choose a colour

This is a game about choices and the consequences of those choices although, in the game, the children have little to base their choices on. It is a fun opening activity which the children can join in as they arrive.

What you need: Coloured rubber mats (suggest twelve) or large pieces of coloured paper or card. CD or tape player, CDs or tapes. Small pieces of coloured card or paper in a container.

What you do:

- Scatter the mats or coloured sheets of paper round the room.
- Children spread out around the room.
- They move around the room as the music is played.
- When the music stops, the children run to stand on one of the coloured mats or sheets of paper.

To make the game more interesting:

- When the music has stopped and the children are on the mats, take a coloured piece of paper out of the box.
- Call out the colour.
- Children on that coloured mat jump up in the air (can explode like a banger with the accompanying sound) and are out.
- They sit at the side.
- Continue until one child is left.
- That child wins a point and, if you have a points system, they also win one for their team.

Bible link

God has chosen us (John 15:16); making choices (Joshua 24:15, Luke 10:42); Abraham and Lot (Genesis 13).

Using the idea

In the game you have to make choices: which mat shall I run to? So it is in life – we have to make choices and, as in the game, we have to live with the consequences of our choice. In the game, are we standing on the colour called? If yes, we stay in the game. If not, we are out. In the game we have little information to base our choice on. The colour called is randomly picked from the box. In life we need to think about all we know that will help us in the choice we make.

The children could divide into groups to talk about the consequences of certain choices, eg bullying, stealing, cheating, lying.

A choice we want the children to make at some time is whether they want to live their lives the Jesus way. Telling the story of Joshua and his declaration, ‘Choose for yourselves this day whom you will serve… But as for me and my household, we will serve the Lord’(Joshua 24:15), leaves the children with the question: who will they serve? Remembering that many of the children in the group may be first contacts, you will have to decide when to turn the question into a personal challenge.

For older children, see also idea 52.

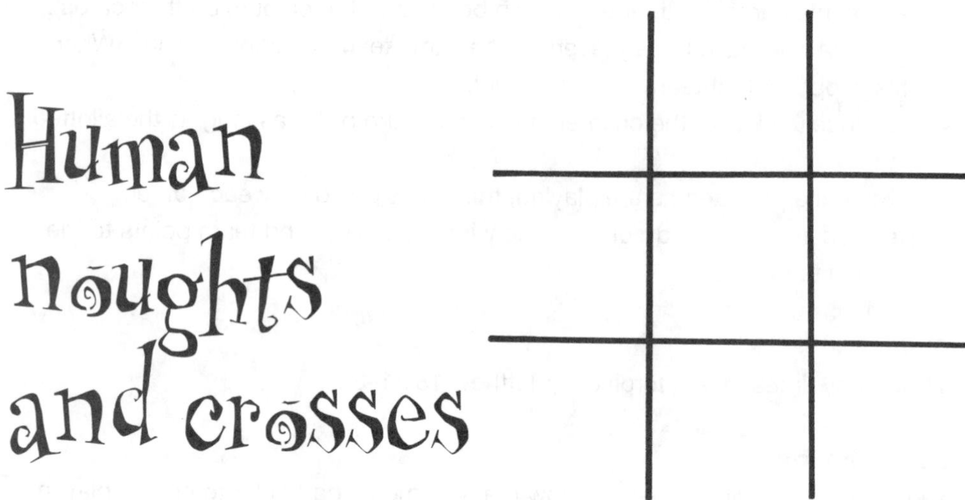

Human noughts and crosses

This game brings a different dimension to the well-known game of noughts and crosses.

What you need: Masking tape.
Cards with O and X or two different coloured cards to denote teams.

What you do:

- Before you play, mark a grid, or grids if more than one team playing at a time, on the floor using masking tape.
- Children line up in (preferably) an even number of teams – either the teams they are usually in, if you have this system, or randomly selected teams. (The teams do not need to be made up of equal numbers.)
- Give one team a nought and the other team a cross or the coloured card denoting their team.

- Explain how to play the game. Each team will take turns at playing. One team will be the 'noughts' the other the 'crosses' (or, if playing in their allocated teams, the names of their teams can be used or the colours on their cards). The idea is to have three players of the same team standing in a line. When this happens, that team scores a point.
- Continue until all of the children have had a turn or for as long as the allotted time.
- If more than two teams are playing, the teams could play each other.
- Keep score and award points to the winning players and team points to the winning team.

Bible link

'How many times must I forgive?' (Matthew 18:21–35).

Using the idea

Keep this fast moving by seeing how many games a particular team can play in the given time. This game is all about:

- Thinking ahead. Choosing where to stand either to block the path of the other team or as part of a strategy move for your team.
- Being accepting and tolerant of others in your team if they choose to stand in a place which you consider to be less helpful to winning the game.
- Being forgiving. You may need to be forgiven yourself sometime. How many times must I forgive? This is a story about God's forgiveness. You could also look at the Lord's Prayer (Matthew 6:9–15).

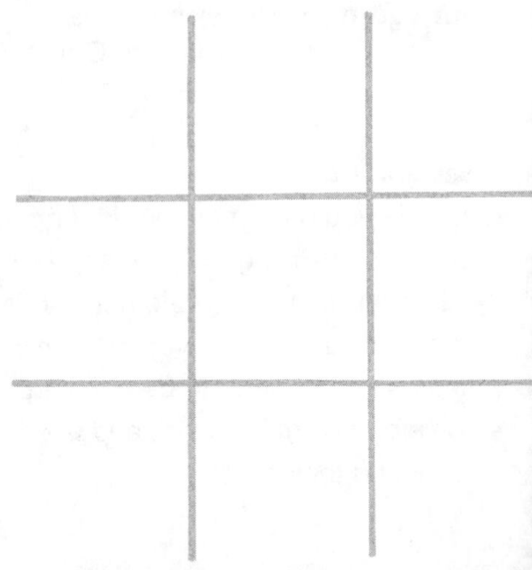

Pass the parcel / Arnold says

Most children enjoy these games. Pass the parcel can introduce the idea of sharing if the prize in the middle is shared. They can both be used to set the scene for 'Who says? Jesus says' and the story of the calling of the first disciples.

1. Pass the parcel

What you need: CD or tape player, CDs or tapes. A parcel (or parcels if playing in teams or with a large number of children), wrapped in lots of layers, with a slip of paper between each layer containing a suggested activity.

Suggestions for activities:

- Touch your nose/ear/knee, etc
- Hop on one leg
- Jump up and down
- Run round the circle
- Turn round

What you do:

- Children sit on the floor in a circle.
- While playing music, pass the parcel round the circle.
- When the music stops, that child unwraps a layer and reads what is written on the interleaved paper.
- Either that child does what it says on the paper, or it's more participative if all of the group do what it says.
- The parcel is then passed round again as the music plays.
- Continue until as many different children as possible have had a turn at unwrapping a layer.
- Share the prize in the middle.

2. Arnold says

A version of 'Simon says'. We had a Simon in our group, so we changed the name and now use 'Arnold says'.

What you do:

- The leader says 'Arnold says …' and then tells the children what to do, eg:
  - Put your hands on your head.
  - Touch your nose with your wrist.
  - Clap your hands.
  - Rub your tummy.
  - Rub your tummy and pat your head at the same time.
- The children only do the action commanded if the leader precedes it with the words 'Arnold says'. If Arnold doesn't say, then the children don't do it.
- This can be played for fun to introduce the teaching or, after a few practice runs, it can be played competitively.
- If playing competitively, watch to see who moves when they shouldn't. These children are 'out' and help to watch the others.
- The winner(s) gets a point, and one for their team if you have this system.

Bible link

Calling the first disciples (Luke 5:1–11); feeding the five thousand (John 6:1–15).

Using the idea

1. After playing pass the parcel you could talk about why the children did the actions that they were doing. The answer is, 'It said on the piece of paper,' or 'The paper said.' Who is it who tells us what to do? Is it Mum or Dad, friends, teachers? For the disciples it was Jesus. They did what Jesus said. Are you willing to do what Jesus says? (See also idea 77.)

2. Talk about sharing as the child who unwrapped the last wrapper shares the prize (which could be mini chocolate bars, biscuits, wrapped sweets, etc) with the other children. The children could be encouraged to say 'thank you' as they take their prize. You may want to tell the story of the boy who shared his lunch with everyone. (See also ideas 30 and 35.)

Ring on a string

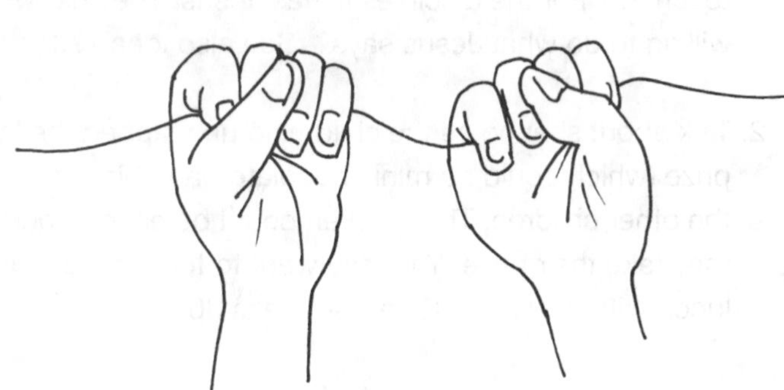

This game involves passing a ring along some string without the ring being seen. The children need to keep their hands moving to look as if they are collecting the ring from the child next to them.

What you need: A length of string for each group.
A ring or Polo mint for each string.

What you do:

- The children stand in a circle holding the string. One child will have hold of the ring.
- One child stands away from the circle, not looking at the children.
- Everyone starts passing the string round pretending that they also have hold of the ring. They need to move their hands to look as if they are collecting the ring from the child next to them.

- The child outside the circle turns and watches as the string is passed round and tries to guess who has the ring.
- If the child guesses correctly, a point is scored and the child who had the ring has a turn at guessing. If this child has already had a turn at guessing, choose another.

Bible link

Andrew tells Simon Peter about Jesus (John 1:40–42).

Using the idea

This game was about passing a ring on without others knowing, but our story is about passing on some news. Andrew had found Jesus. He had been to his house and spent the day with him (John 1:39). It had been fantastic and he didn't want to keep that news to himself. He immediately rushed off to tell his brother, Simon Peter, all about his day and the new friend he had made. Andrew had found the Messiah, the Christ, and he took his brother to meet him.

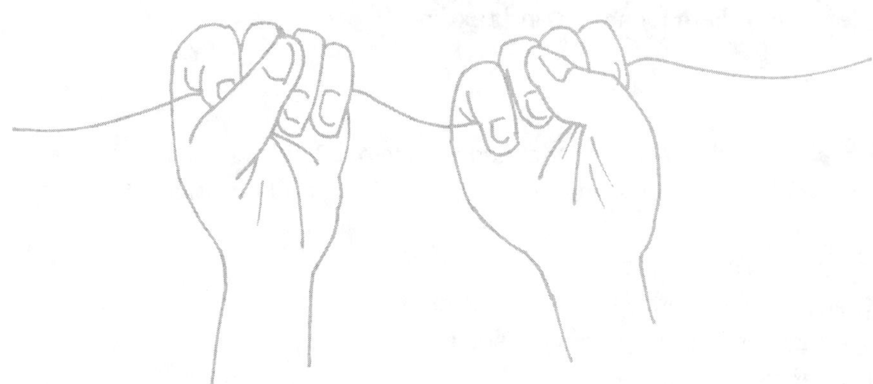

Pass the Sock

This game makes use of our sense of touch. Items are placed into the sock and the children find them by placing one hand in the sock and identifying them by shape and texture.

What you need: A sock for each team. Sets of 20 items for each sock, eg. penny, wool, paper clip, stamp, thimble, teaspoon, ribbon, rubber, etc.

What you do:

- Children sit in a circle in their teams or groups.
- They take it in turns to hold the sock.
- Leader calls out an item.
- The child with the sock puts his or her hand inside and pulls out the named object.
- The first to hold the object up wins a point.

- The child then replaces the item and passes the sock on to the next player.
- Continue passing the sock round until all have had a turn.
- Add up points for each team.

Bible link

Blind Bartimaeus (Mark 10:46–52); lost and found (Luke 15); hidden treasure (Matthew 13:44–46).

Using the idea

Tell the children that the objects in the sock were hidden. To find the correct object, they had to feel around for it and identify it by using their sense of touch. This could be linked to a blind person. Talk about how they use their senses of touch and hearing to help them to find things. Tell the story of Blind Bartimaeus (Mark 10:46–52).

Another application is to take the lost and found stories in Luke 15 and talk about looking for something when you don't know where it is. For the sheep, the shepherd went out into the open country to hunt for the sheep. He looked behind the boulders, in the bushes, on the ledges – everywhere he could think of until he found his sheep. The woman lit a lamp to help her find her lost coin. She searched carefully, getting her broom out to brush into the corners, moving the furniture until she found it. The father of the lost son watched the road every day for his son's return. Each of them celebrated the finding of that which they had lost. We may think God doesn't know about us or where we are, but he does, and he sent Jesus to find us and to help us.

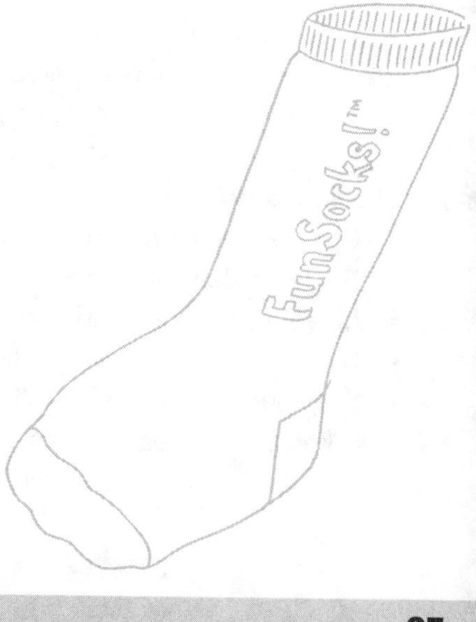

Parachute crossovers

This makes a good opening activity. The children join in as they arrive and are quickly involved. The game can be finished as soon as you want as the children will all have had turns.

What you need: A play parachute.
A paper and pen to keep a record of calls.

What you do:

- Children gather round parachute.
- Review safety (see page 281).
- Move parachute up and down.
- Mushroom parachute by lifting it and taking a step forward.
- Step back as parachute falls.
- When you are ready to play, the leader calls out a random selection of
  - colours that the children might be wearing;

  - ages;
  - type of footwear (shoes, trainers);
  - something they've eaten today;
  - initial letters of names;
  - letters in your name.
- Children who qualify run under the parachute.
- Check to see if the children really do qualify.

Bible link

The story of Naaman (2 Kings 5); Joshua and Caleb (Numbers 13:30–33).

Using the idea

1. Dip in the river

Include in the game that the first child to run under the parachute seven times is the winner. Tell the children that seven was an important number for a man called Naaman. He had a skin disease called leprosy and when he went to see Elisha about it, Elisha told him to wash himself seven times in the River Jordan. He wasn't too happy about this as the river didn't look very clean. His servants persuaded him to do what Elisha, who was a prophet (a man of God), had said. When he did, he was healed of his leprosy.

2. How big?

Joshua and Caleb were all for going into the Promised Land. Caleb said, "We should go up and take possession of the land, for we can certainly do it." But the men who had gone up with him said, "We can't attack those people; they are stronger than we are." And they spread among the Israelites [the people] a bad report about the land they had explored. The people believed this report with the result that none of those people ever went into the land God had promised to them. The people of Israel spent the next forty years wandering around in the wilderness. However, God honoured Joshua and Caleb and they did get to go into the Promised Land. The result of not telling the truth can not only affect us but it can affect many around us who believe what we say. (See also idea 77.)

Parachute football / Popcorn

Children enjoy playing parachute football but it is tiring to keep going over a long period of time. We have found the first to five is a good length of time and, if this is reached quickly, leaves energy for a second game to equalise. The decider can follow later if the goals are a long time in coming. This is a competitive game more suited to older children.

Alternatively, Popcorn is a non-competitive game that both younger and older children will enjoy. The game is played by bouncing small, light plastic balls up and down on the parachute until all the balls have bounced off. Spectacular and great fun!

1. Parachute football

What you need: A play parachute.
Indoor footballs in two different colours.

What you do:

- Children stand round the parachute, holding the edge in both hands.
- Divide the children into teams – easiest for scoring is boys versus girls or give coloured cards or bands to one or both teams. Use two different coloured balls.
- Move the parachute up and down, bouncing the balls on the parachute.
- Goals are scored when that team's ball goes through the centre hole or, should the parachute not have a centre hole, until the ball bounces off the parachute.
- First to five wins.
- Moving the parachute gently or vigorously and then lifting it up or down can be used to advantage.

2. Popcorn

What you need: A parachute or king-sized bed sheet.
Small, lightweight plastic balls (one for each child or as many as you may choose to use).

What you do:

- Children stand round the parachute holding on to the edge.
- Give each child a different coloured ball.
- Get the parachute moving gently up and down.
- The children throw their balls onto the parachute and start to move it vigorously up and down as they watch the balls bounce off.
- At the end of the game, the children can collect a ball and the game can be repeated.
- When the game is over, the children collect a ball and place it in the container that you have for them.

Bible link

Jesus stills the storm (Luke 8:22–24); Paul shipwrecked (Acts 27:27–44).

Using the idea

Use the movements of the parachute to talk about the storm and, in contrast, the water being calm and still. (See also idea 77.)

Parachute cat and mouse / sharks

Two popular parachute games.

What you need: A play parachute.

What you do:

1. Cat and mouse

- Children stand round the parachute. Those who want to play take off their shoes.
- Choose one child to be a cat and three to be mice. The mice go under the parachute, the cat goes on top of the parachute.
- The other children move the parachute gently up and down while the cat tries to catch the mice by touching them through the parachute.
- When a mouse is caught, he or she joins the rest of the children round the parachute.

- When all mice are caught, or time is up, a new cat and new mice are chosen.

Choose similar sized children to play each time so the 'mice' are not hurt.

2. Sharks

- The children sit round the parachute.
- If they want to play, they take off their shoes and sit with their legs under the parachute.
- Choose three children to be the sharks. They go under the parachute.
- The other children move the parachute up and down.
- When a 'shark' touches a child's feet, he or she changes places, becomes a shark and goes underneath the parachute.

Be careful the 'sharks' don't pull the children under the parachute as, especially on a shiny surface, the children could bump their heads.

Bible link

The paralysed man (Mark 2:1–12); the Good Samaritan (Luke 10:30–37); Jesus at Bethany (John 12:1–3).

Using the idea

Talk about enjoying the game but caring for each other. You could tell the story of people who cared for other people in the Bible, eg the paralysed man whose friends cared for him; the Good Samaritan, who cared for the man who had been attacked by robbers; Mary and Martha who cared for Jesus by providing him with food and refreshing his feet with the perfume. (See also ideas 25 and 34.)

Section Two: **Craft Activities**

Craft is an excellent way to get alongside children and to listen as they make something. It can also make an excellent opening activity, which children can join in with as they arrive. It gives a focus to the session and can have a calming influence. The activities can be done for their own sake and do not have to be linked in to a Bible theme, but Bible links are included where appropriate should you be looking for one.

FOR ALL CRAFT ACTIVITIES

Make sure the floor and tables are suitably protected. It is worth investing in polythene sheeting which can be placed under tables to protect carpets and floors.

Aprons should be worn for messy activities like those involving clay, glue, paint, permanent felt pens, etc.

Hand washing after activities can be a messy affair too, especially if children have to open doors to get to the wash basins. A bowl of water available near the activity may take off the worst before the children wash their hands properly.

Ask children to write their name on their work, or provide pieces of paper for the children to label their work

Making caterpillars

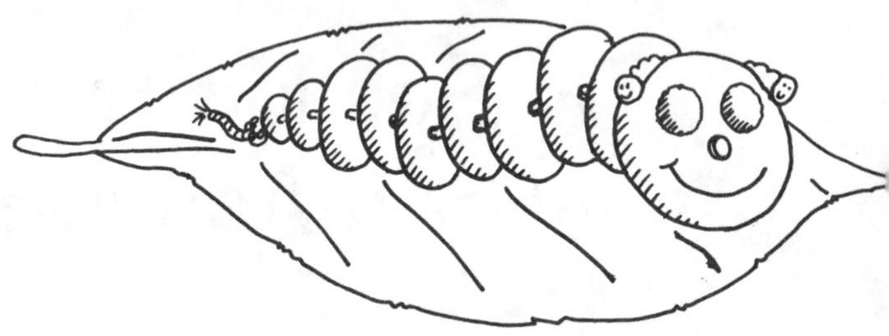

This can be included in the programme in the autumn when there are a lot of conkers around, or use beads during the caterpillar season.

What you need: Conkers or large beads – five conkers or seven beads, depending on size, for each child.

Small beads or googly eyes (available in craft shops) – two for each child.

Green card cut into leaf shapes.

Glue with enough glue spreaders for one each or one between two.

Glitter (optional).

What you do:

- Children put on aprons.
- Explain to the children what they are going to make and show them 'one you made earlier'.
- Give each child a leaf-shaped piece of card and ask them to write their name on it.
- The children need to think about where on the leaf they want to have their caterpillar. They then glue on their first conker (or bead).
- They continue to glue the conkers (or beads) onto the card until they have a line of conkers.
- Dab two tiny blobs of glue onto the conker (or bead) at one end of the line. Place two small beads or googly eyes on these. The caterpillar now has a head with a face.
- Dab glue onto the surface of the caterpillar and shake glitter over (optional).
- Leave to dry.

Bible link

The plague of locusts (Exodus 10:1–20).

Using the idea

Talk to the children about the caterpillars they have made. Ask them, 'What do caterpillars do all day?' One answer is, 'They eat leaves.' There was a bigger creature than a caterpillar in the Bible that loved to eat leaves. It was called a locust. (You may like to show a picture of a locust.) These came in swarms and would quickly eat a field of crops. God sent a plague of locusts over the country of Egypt to persuade Pharaoh to let the Israelite people go. Tell the story from Exodus 10. (See also ideas 18, 29, 42 and 79.)

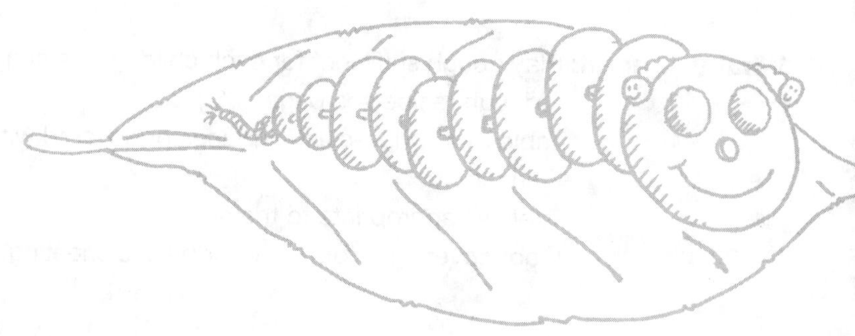

Using play dough

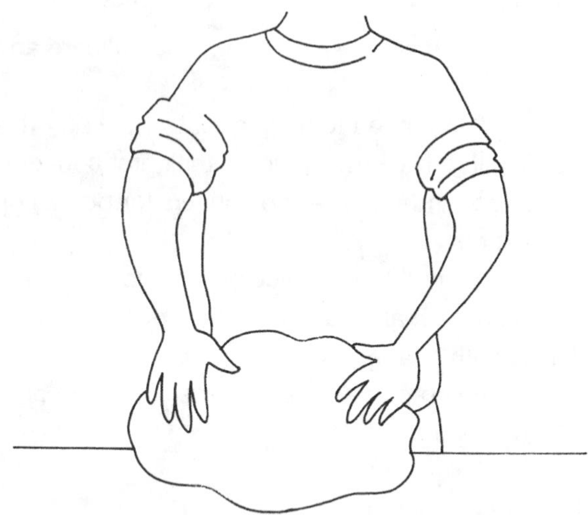

Always popular. The children can be asked to create something of their choosing or they can be asked to make something specific to link with the teaching of the session. It is a good idea to cover the floor with an old sheet or plastic sheeting if the floor is carpeted or needs protecting.

What you need: Play dough sufficient for each child. (For a suggested play dough recipe see page 283.)

Tables with wipe-clean surfaces or covered with plastic sheets.

Tools as appropriate to the activity.

Floor coverings – old sheet or plastic sheeting.

What you do:

- Give out the play dough for the children to play with.
- As they only have a short time, tell them that in a few minutes you would like to see what they have made.
- Encourage the children to look at each other's models.
- Put away the play dough.

Bible link

Story of Creation (Genesis 1).

Using the idea

Talk about how God created the earth and all that is in it. Tell the children that we are made in God's image and therefore God has made us to be creative too. Thank him together that we can make things. (See also ideas 13 and 14.)

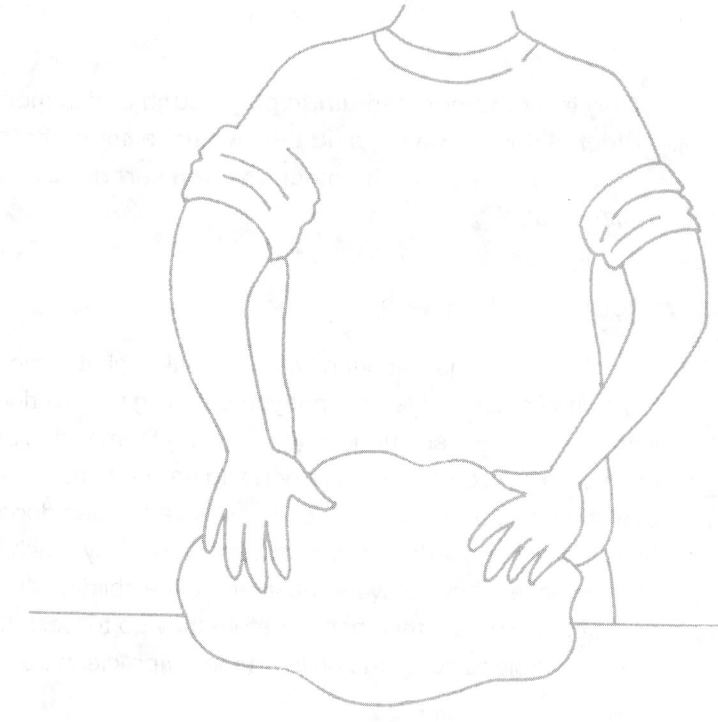

Clay modelling

Clay is a different medium to play dough and is more challenging for older children. Having said this, we have set up both play dough and clay as choices and the older children surprised us by choosing the play dough!

Children do enjoy working with clay, although it is more messy for the hands, table and floor. Don't let this put you off using it. Covering the floor, using tables with easy wipe-clean surfaces (or covering them with plastic sheeting), or giving each child a piece of waxed paper, and having hand-washing facilities nearby will overcome this problem. If the children have to open doors and turn on taps before they can wash their hands, everything they touch will become covered in clay, so have a bowl of water near where the children are working for getting the worst of the clay off their hands before they go to wash their hands properly. It is also advisable to cover the children too. Wipe-clean aprons are ideal, or we often use white bin liners, tearing holes in the top for the head and in the sides for the children's arms. These are inexpensive and disposable. We explain to the children what we are doing and hold the bag closely together as we pass it over their heads so that there is no fear of suffocation for them.

Two ideas follow but there are many different ways in which clay can be used as an activity for its own sake or to be the focus for Bible teaching.

What you need: Clay – sufficient for each child. This can be purchased from shops like the Early Learning Centre.
Aprons for the children.
Coverings for the floor and tables.
Bowl for washing the worst of the clay off the children's hands.
Paper towels or kitchen roll for drying hands.
Paper bags – these can be bought in a Cash-and-Carry or, with warning so they can buy them in for you, from a friendly newsagent.
Clay-marking instruments (can be spoons).
Models made beforehand as examples.

1. A pot

What you do:

- Show the children the pot that you have made.
- Demonstrate different ways of making pots out of clay – thumb pots (made by rolling the clay into a ball and then pushing thumb into the middle to make a hollow), or coil pots (made by rolling the clay into a long 'sausage' and then coiling the clay round and round to make the base and then coiling up to make the sides of the pot).
- Give the children a piece of clay each and encourage them to create their own pots.
- The pots can be decorated with marks made by the clay-marking instruments or by using the end of a spoon.
- If the children are taking their pots home, you could first display them on named paper bags. This will also allow the pots to dry out a little before they are placed in the bags.

Bible link

The potter's house (Jeremiah 18:1–6).

Using the idea

Talk about how pots are made and how this applies to our lives. The potter would take the clay and pound it – life hurts sometimes.

The potter has to work with the clay, not against it. He lifts it and pounds it to get all the air bubbles out.

In the story, Jeremiah is watching the potter mould the clay into the shape he wants it. As he watches, he understands that this is what God wants to do with our lives. He wants to mould and shape us into the kind of person he wants. As the clay is strengthened by being pounded, so too are we being made stronger as we face new experiences.

The potter puts the clay in the middle of the wheel. It's important for us to be in the middle of God's will or we will turn out misshapen. To keep our lives going in the right direction, we need to live in the way the Bible tells us – the Jesus way.

2. Nightlight holders

What you need: In addition to the list above you will also need nightlight candles – one for each child.

What you do:

- Show the children one that you made earlier to give them an idea of what they are doing.
- Give each child some clay and a nightlight.
- Encourage them to design their own, using the nightlight to help them to mould and shape the holder.
- When they have made their holder they can complete their design using the clay-marking instruments and cutters.
- Allow to dry.

ADDITIONAL IDEA

Once dry, the finished nightlight holder or pot can be painted or varnished.

What you need: Ready-mix paint and paintbrushes.
PVA glue to varnish (optional).

Bible link

Light of Christ (John 1:4–5); the lamp of the body (Luke 11:33–36); the ten bridesmaids (Matthew 25:1–13).

Using the idea

Talk about Jesus' coming into the world as being like light coming into a dark room. The world was dark because it was without God. It had religion but the people were not living in the way God had planned. Jesus came into the world to show people the way to live. This could be used with the candle dance described in idea 90 to the song *'The Light Of Christ'.*

The story in Luke 11 talks about our eyes bringing light into our body. You may want to talk to the children about what they see on television, on videos, in comics or magazines. Is all that they are watching good for them to see? Are they strong enough to turn the television off if they are unhappy about the programme? Can they say 'no' to reading an unsuitable magazine?

Songs on this theme: *'I will be yours'* from Doug Horley's album *Whoopah Wahey!* This was written to encourage children to think a bit more about what they are watching on television. Another song is *'The TV Song'* from Ishmael's *Songs for Little Children*. Both these albums are available from Children's Ministry.

The story of the ten bridesmaids is about being ready for Jesus. A possible challenge for the children.

Modelling with coloured clay

Coloured modelling clay is brilliant to use as it is not messy and the end result is so colourful and effective. With our mid-week group, called BUGZ, we used it early on in our launch programme to help the children to identify with the group and to be creative. The modelling clay can, of course, be used to create anything of your choice, but this idea is for bugs.

What you need: Coloured modelling clay.
Aprons.
Wipe-clean tables, or table offerings.
Paper bags for taking models home.

What you do:

- Give each child small pieces of modelling clay in a selection of colours.
- Challenge the children to design a bug.
- Display the bugs on named paper bags.

Bible link

Bugs in Egypt (Exodus 8, 10).

Using the idea

Ask the children, 'Did you know there are bugs in the Bible?' They may be able to tell you where. Tell the story from Exodus of the plagues of frogs, gnats, flies (Exodus 8), and locusts (Exodus 10). Pharaoh would not listen to Moses' requests but God was on Moses' side. He sent plagues so that Pharaoh would know that he was God – all-powerful and a force to be reckoned with.

This story carries on until Pharaoh gives in after the death of his eldest son. You could continue to tell it over a few weeks, talking about the Passover (Exodus 12:1–30), and the Exodus (Exodus 12:31–42). Craft activities for future weeks could include making bread without yeast (see idea 36), the game 'In the river, on the bank' (idea 2), or the dance drama in idea 79.

Animal masks

Masks can help the children participate in the story. These can be attached to the head with elastic or simply held in front of the face. This example is held in front of the face. Animals make good characters for masks.

What you need: A paper plate for each child.
Cotton wool (for sheep) and orange wool (for lions).
PVA glue and glue sticks.
Felt pens.
Lolly sticks and sticky tape (optional).
One made earlier as an example.

What you do:

- Talk to the children about what they are making and show them an example.
- Give each child a paper plate and ask them to write their name on the back.
- Draw in eyes and mouth. The eyes do not need to be cut out.
- Glue on cotton wool for sheep or orange wool for lion.
- Optional: attach the top half of a lolly stick to the back of the plate with sticky tape to form a 'handle'.
- The mask is now ready to use for the story later in the session.

Bible link

Lost sheep (Luke 15:3–7); Daniel in the lions' den (Daniel 6).

Using the idea

Tell your chosen story with the children taking part wearing their masks. (See also ideas 54 and 70.)

Colouring a picture

This makes an easy opening activity. The picture for colouring could be linked to the Bible story or to the name of the group.

What you need: Paper or photocopied pictures.
Felt pens.

What you do: We used pictures from *A Bug's Life* for our group BUGZ when it first began in order to encourage group identity. If you have access to a computer, a print studio package or non-copyright Clip Art can provide the pictures you need. These can then be photocopied.

The children can also create their own pictures. We held a competition for the best group mascot bug. These pictures were then displayed, the winners were given computer-scanned copies of their bug as their prize and the best one was used by the group as its mascot.

Bible link

Exodus 8 and 10.

Using the idea

The picture provides the focus for the story. We asked the children, 'Did you know there were bugs in the Bible?' (based on Exodus 8 [gnats, flies] and 10 [locusts]) as described in idea 15. (See also ideas 14 and 50.)

Making a mural

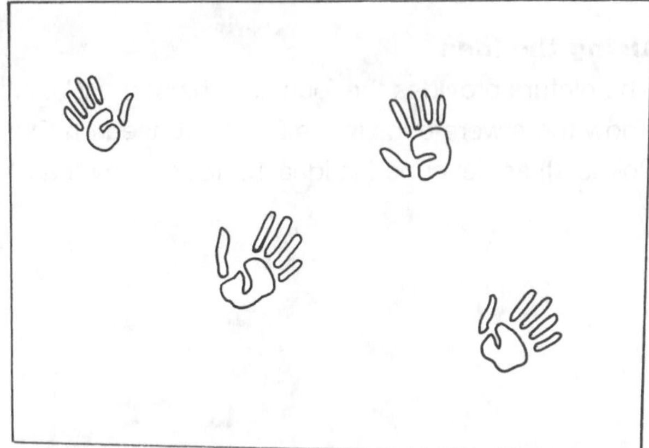

This makes an excellent opening activity as the children join in as they arrive. The picture can be linked to the theme for the day.

What you need: A roll of paper for each team.
Felt pens.

What you do:

As the children arrive, they draw pictures on the paper, linked to the theme for the session, to make one large mural or frieze.

Bible link

The Creation (Genesis 1:11, 20–24); harvest time (Ruth 2); the Good Samaritan (Luke 10:30–37); the ten lepers (Luke 17:11–19).

Using the idea

Use the finished picture to help you tell the story. The story can be read aloud, dramatised, shown on video or however you choose.

A possible theme might be the family. Who is in your family? The children can draw and name themselves and the members of their family. You could talk about caring for one another in our families. Tell them that the club is a bit like a family and talk about caring for one another there.

For the theme of harvest the children can draw different produce – not just from the land and sea, but also what is made in towns from the resources of the land. Talk about all that we have and all God has provided. You may want to talk about how we care for the world and how we share all its wealth around. At the moment the sharing is unfair.

Another approach is to tell the story of Ruth as you look at how the grain was harvested in Bible times, or you could introduce this story as one told at harvest time – 'The story with the happy ending'.

For a theme of hands, see how many hands each team can fit onto the paper in the given time – count for the winning team. Later the talk can be about hands and how we can use them to be kind and to do things that God would be pleased about. Tell the story of the Good Samaritan.

Alternatively, the children can be asked to draw a picture of something they are thankful for. This could be used to introduce the story of the ten lepers, when only one said thank you. Finish with short 'thank you' prayers.

Rubbings

Children enjoy seeing an image appear as they rub over the paper held on the object. It is important to keep the paper still, so using masking tape to tape the paper down may help. Choose objects to fit your theme.

What you need: Paper.
Wax crayons.
Objects for rubbing, eg coins, bricks, bark of tree, templates of animals or vehicles.
Masking tape (optional).

What you do:

- Give each child a piece of paper and ask them to write their name on the paper.

- Give each child an object.
- Children place paper over object to be rubbed, fixing with masking tape if required.
- Rub wax crayon over paper to reveal the texture or pattern on the object.

Bible link

Story of the lost coin (Luke 15:8–10); the greedy taxman (Luke 19:1–10); making bricks in Egypt (Exodus 5:6–9).

Using the idea

Use the rubbing as a focus for telling the Bible story.

1. The lost coin

If the children use rubbings of coins, ask them about the coins. Were they 10p, 2p, 1p, 5p, 20p, 50p? To introduce the story, ask the children, 'How would you feel if these coins were yours and you lost one?'

Well, this happened to a lady in the Bible. She was counting her coins when she found one was missing. Each coin was worth about a day's wage. Houses in those times often had no windows and floors made of earth. This made it very difficult to find a coin. So, what did she do? She lit a lamp, swept the house and searched carefully. She looked under the bed, behind the cupboard, round the potted plant, under the cat, in the corners, along the skirting boards, down the sides of the sofa (not sure they really had furniture like this in those days!). She looked under the mat, among the pans, and in the cracks in the floor. She looked with her lamp, brushed with her broom and searched and searched until she found her lost coin and when she found it... she called her friends and held a party.

(See also ideas 30, 31 and 78.)

2. The greedy taxman

Ask the children, 'What do you think about money?'

Lots of people don't think they have enough money. A man called Zacchaeus was a bit like that. He worked for the Romans who were a foreign occupying force. He was a Jew and his job was to collect taxes from his fellow Jews to give to the Romans – well, someone had to do it. The problem was, Zacchaeus liked the sound and the feel of the money. He got an idea. If he added on a bit extra to everyone's tax bill, there would be more money for him. After all, he was due a pay rise and the Romans were hardly likely to give him one.

Well, this went on for years and he was making quite a tidy sum. No one liked him very much but that didn't bother him. It hadn't taken them long to work out what he was doing. Then one day his life changed. He had got up as usual and was demanding money from people and seeming to be very authoritative so nobody would argue with him – after all, he had the backing of the Roman army.

There was some shouting outside. He couldn't stand noise, it spoilt his concentration. He went out to see what all the fuss was about. 'Jesus is coming! Jesus is coming!' was what the people were shouting. He had heard about Jesus and wanted to see him so he pushed his way through the crowd. The crowd pushed back. They wanted to see Jesus too. So Zacchaeus ran on ahead and climbed a sycamore-fig tree, a sturdy tree with a short trunk and branches that spread out. Easy to climb into and ideal for sitting in. He could see Jesus coming.

Then to Zacchaeus's surprise, Jesus stopped under his tree, looked up and told him that he must come down immediately because Jesus was coming to stay at his house. Well, the people were shocked – didn't Jesus know that this man was a cheat? They would soon tell him if he didn't. But Jesus knew what he was doing. Before you knew it, Zacchaeus was owning up to Jesus about his cheating and getting money for himself that wasn't his – a bit like stealing – and he was promising to give the money back with interest and to give away half of what he owned to the poor. Zacchaeus's life had changed because for the first time someone had believed in him enough to be a guest in his house. He realised that he didn't like the person he was. Being greedy for money was not the answer to the good life. He had a nice house and would have had a cool car if cars had been invented, but there is more to life than money. He was lonely. He was empty inside. What brought the change? He met with Jesus.

3. Bricks in Egypt

If the children take rubbings of bricks, look at the rubbings, look at the bricks – colour and texture. Feel the weight of them. Ask them if they know how bricks are made today.

In Bible times, bricks were made out of mud mixed with chopped straw and left in the sun to dry. In our story the people of God, who were called the Israelites, were slaves in Egypt and the Egyptians made them make bricks.

The Israelites asked the Egyptian king if they could go into the desert and worship their God, but the Egyptian king didn't like the Israelites and he said, 'No. If you've got time to go off and worship your God then you have too much time. Make bricks without straw.' That was impossible. What he really meant was, 'Go and gather your own straw.' So that is what they had to do. One problem: the Egyptian king still ordered them to make as many bricks as before but now they had less time to do it, and if they didn't reach the number the Israelite foremen were beaten.

Something's not fair here. The Israelite foremen knew they were in trouble and went to see Moses. They blamed him for all their trouble. So Moses talked to God.

The story continues in Exodus 6. (See also idea 79.)

Making mats

One way of keeping rubbings is to make them into mats or coasters. These can be attractive and the children feel they have made something that can be used.

What you need: Items to rub, eg small templates of animals, or natural objects like leaves, bark.
Paper.
Wax crayons.
Coloured card.
Scissors.
PVA glue.

What you do:

- Place a piece of paper over the object to be rubbed.
- Rub a crayon over the paper until the shape of the object appears.
- Cut out the rubbing and glue onto the card.
- Cover the card with PVA glue. Leave to dry.
- These can be used as mats for standing drinks on tables.

Bible link

Creation (Genesis 1).

Using the idea

You may like to tell the story first and then talk to the children about their choice of rubbings. When dry, the rubbings can be taken home and used as table mats for cold drinks.

Paint a letter

Painting is a popular, albeit potentially messy, activity. Painting letters should be less messy than free painting as the children paint between the lines of the letter on pre-prepared cards. These can be hand-drawn or computer generated using an open font. They do not need to be cut out. The children in our club did manage to paint without making too much mess and they were very careful how they painted their letters. Thick felt pens could be used if you prefer. The letters could make up the name of the group or the Bible verse for display.

What you need: Prepared letters on A4 paper or card for the children to paint within the lines.
Paint and brushes.
Aprons.
Plastic covered or wipe-clean tables.

What you do:

- Give each child a letter.
- Ask them to paint it carefully within the lines.
- Leave to dry.
- When dry, arrange the letters into words for display. This could be for group meetings, a church service to introduce the congregation to the group, or for a game to sort out the order of the letters.

Using the idea

This idea can be used to display a Bible verse for the session or to memorise. This could be done by either getting the children to hold the cards or, if holes are already punched into the cards, threading them onto string in the correct order. The children say the verse together.

Alternatively you can use the cards for a game. The children move round to music and when the music stops they must get into line so their team's letters spell out the word.

Painting on wood

Few children have painted on wood and so they can become really excited about this activity as they pick up their paint-brush. Because this is a new medium for most children, allowing them to paint as they choose releases their creativity. You can choose either to paint on a piece of wood, which is similar to painting on paper, or to decorate an object like a wooden spoon.

What you need: Hard wood pre-cut into suitable sizes and shapes and with the edges sanded smooth.
Paint and paintbrushes.
PVA glue or varnish (optional).

What you do:

- Give each child a small piece of prepared wood, and a paintbrush.
- Unless you have a theme that you want to set for the painting, let the children paint and you'll be surprised at their creativity.
- When the paintings are dry, they can be varnished over with PVA glue or varnish to seal the paint, if required.

Bible link

The Crucifixion (Luke 23:26–43); the feeding of the five thousand (Luke 9:10–17); breakfast on the beach (John 21:1–14); a lost sheep (Luke 15:1–7); Daniel in the lions' den (Daniel 6).

Using the idea

Older children may be able to illustrate a Bible story on their piece of wood, so before they start painting tell them a story. One idea is to tell the children about Jesus' death on a cross and the others who died with him. They could paint three crosses, maybe on a hill, on their piece of wood. Or tell a story about fish, sheep or other animals. Have simple and fun pictures of animals to help the children with their paintings.

Younger children are best left to paint as they choose. You may find that they add one colour onto another with the finished picture being a muddy brown colour. This in itself does not look so attractive to adults but may be a masterpiece for the child.

When the pictures are dry they can be linked to a Bible story by adding a colourful sticker of a sheep, pig, cow or lion. (Shops like the Early Learning Centre often have boxes of animal stickers.) Alternatively use a sticker with a Bible verse on it to relate to the story being told.

ADDITIONAL IDEA

The same can be done with a wooden spoon or brush. As the surface is smaller, and the shape is already clear, let the children decorate it as they choose. This is most likely to be with a pattern. You may need to sandpaper the objects carefully before painting and, as with the pictures, they can be varnished when dry to make them waterproof.

Bible link

Martha in the kitchen (Luke 10:38–42).

Using the idea

Tell the story of Martha in the kitchen. You may want to concentrate on the kitchen side of the story thereby including the spoon and stirring the food. This could be dramatised as you tell the children that Martha has so much to do, there is flour in her hair, water spilt on the floor. She wants everything to be just right for Jesus but she is still busy in the kitchen, stirring her pots and baking her bread, when he arrives. Mary leaves her to go to Jesus and poor Martha is left, rather frustrated, to finish everything off by herself. She is rather annoyed and says to Jesus, 'Don't you care that my sister has left me to do all the work by myself? Tell her to help me!' Jesus doesn't help by sending Mary to her. He gently suggests that Martha leaves the kitchen and joins them.

Tie dye

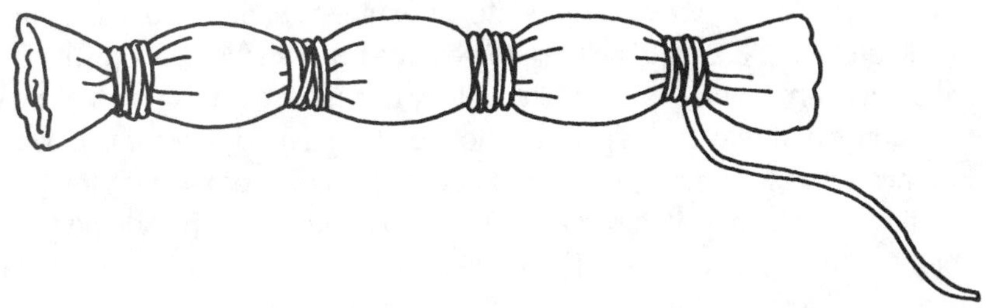

All sorts of items can be decorated with tie dye, including belts, headbands, scarves and T-shirts. When the item is dry it's possible to tie dye again with another colour. Children love this activity but it is potentially very messy. As it takes more time, it makes an ideal workshop activity, particularly for older children.

What you need: Disposable rubber gloves (optional).
Cotton T-shirt or strips of material.
Tie dye.
Bowls for dye and cold water.
Elastic bands; string; newspaper.

What you do:

- Children wear aprons and disposable gloves (optional).
- Tie material by placing your finger (pointing upright) under the material and wrapping an elastic band tightly around it.
- Remove your finger, move to another section of material and continue to wrap elastic bands in a similar way, in the design of your choice.
- Once all the elastic bands are in place, attach a piece of string to an elastic band near the end of the material and place into the dye making sure that the string is hanging outside the container.
- Leave it for the given time on the tie dye instructions (usually about 4 minutes).
- Remove and place on newspaper.
- Leave to dry.
- When dry, undo all elastic bands and iron if required (you may want the children to do this at home.)

Bible link

The body of Christ (1 Corinthians 12:12–13); one in Christ (Galatians 3:28).

Using the idea

Tie dyeing is a good focus for thinking about the bright colours worn by people in a country like South America and could be included in a project about other countries of the world. Other activities might include making and eating food from different countries. This idea can also be linked with idea 24.

You might talk about accepting people who choose different ways of dressing, or who choose different colours of clothes. Some of the children in the group may love the idea of wearing what they have made; others may not like it, but can learn to be accepting of other people's choices.

This could lead in to talking about people who may dress differently, speak differently or eat different foods from us and to recognise that, deep down, God has made us all the same. We all have feelings and need families, friends, homes, food and clean water to drink. We all need to be loved and cared for and it hurts just the same if other people are not nice to us.

Should you wish to look at clothes in Bible times for a special project, information can be found in *The Lion Encyclopaedia of the Bible* (Lion Publishing).

Pebble paperweights

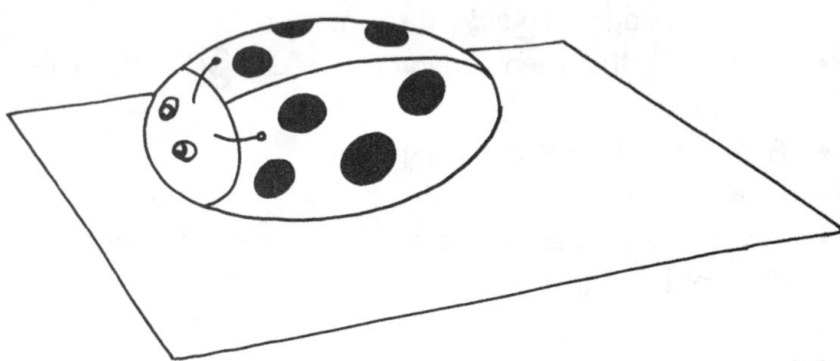

Pebbles are another fun medium for painting. They can be made into paperweights as gifts by painting them and then maybe adding stickers when dry, to give a Christian message. The following suggests transforming them into ladybirds or spiders

What you need: One pebble for each child.
Paint and paintbrushes.
Moving eyes (optional); black stickers for spots on ladybird.
Cover for table, and aprons for children.

What you do:

- Children paint pebble red with a black head for a ladybird, or brown with a black head for a spider.
- Leave to dry.

- When dry, stick black spots on like a ladybird's markings. Black paper legs can be added to make the spiders.

Optional:

- Paint over the stones lightly with PVA glue to seal.
- Add eyes.
- Add a Christian sticker.

Bible link

Noah's Ark (Genesis 6–8); Martha's kitchen (Luke 10:38–42); the Prodigal Son's pig sty (Luke 15:11–27); Daniel in the lions' den (Daniel 6).

Using the idea

Tell a story, using the pictures on the pebbles as a focus and to make the relevant teaching point. The story of the Prodigal Son could be told, for example, through the eyes of a spider:

I was spinning my web in the corner when I saw this young man. He was new about the pig sty and he didn't look too happy. His clothes were too smart for the job. He looked as though he was more used to the high life than the pig sty. He did his job well though – feeding the pigs – but what a dirty and smelly job it was!

I was asleep one night when his talking woke me up. By now his clothes were a bit tatty and I thought, 'Who's he talking to?' Himself, I suppose, as the pigs were asleep. He was talking about his life and remembering another farm. 'Sounds better than this,' I thought, and so did he. He was thinking about going back to it. Wondering what his old dad would say. Well, next day he was off. I wonder what happened when he got home. I would like to be the fly on the wall for that home-coming – or perhaps I should say 'the spider in the web'!

The story of Mary and Martha could be told through the eyes of a ladybird resting on the window sill, or the story of Noah's Ark or Daniel re-told in a similar way depending on your choice of creature for the paperweight.

Alternatively the message on the sticker can be the focus for the Bible teaching.

Making bead jewellery

This has to have been the most popular activity with girls this year – making bracelets, anklets and necklaces out of beads. Bracelets and anklets are preferable as these use fewer beads per child, and necklaces also need safety beads at each end. Sets of beads purchased usually include a pair of safety beads.

What you need: Beads and a supply of thin elastic.

What you do:

- Cut the elastic to suitable lengths for the choice of jewellery (eg: bracelet, anklet).

- Knot one end.
- The children choose beads and thread these onto the elastic.
- When the elastic is covered, knot the open end.
- Tie the two ends together.
- The jewellery is ready to wear.

Bible link
The lost coin (Luke 15:8–10).

Using the idea
Talk about jewellery in Bible times and how important it was for this woman to find her missing coin. The coins were probably her dowry, worn as a headdress or necklace. Information on jewellery in Bible times can be found in *The Lion Encyclopaedia of the Bible* (Lion Publishing). (See also idea 22.)

Acetate greetings cards

Acetate cards provide a different medium to work with and give a pleasing effect. They can be used as greetings cards to show how we care for friends or family.

What you need: A5 coloured card – one for each child.
A selection of suitable pictures (animals, fish, birds, flowers, etc) photocopied onto acetate sheets and cut out.
Permanent felt pens.
Pre-cut aluminium foil.
PVA glue or gluesticks.
Aprons.

What you do:

- Children put aprons on. (Very important as the ink from these pens will not wash out.)
- Give each child a piece of A5 card and a small piece of aluminium foil.
- Let them choose an acetate picture.
- Children colour the acetate picture using the permanent felt pens. While the pictures are drying, fold the card.
- Glue aluminium foil onto the front of the card, checking that the card opens the right way.
- Glue the acetate picture onto the aluminium foil.
- Add an appropriate greeting inside the card.

Bible link

The lost sheep (Luke 15:1–7); the wedding at Cana (John 2:1–11); Mary and Martha (Luke 10:38–42); Mary anoints Jesus' feet (John 12:1–3); Jesus washes the disciples' feet (John 13:12–15).

Using the idea

All the people in these Bible stories demonstrated that they cared. The shepherd cared enough to go and look for his sheep; Jesus' mother cared that they had run out of wine at the wedding; Martha cared enough to cook a meal for Jesus; Mary cared enough to anoint Jesus' feet with perfume; and Jesus cared enough to wash his disciples' feet. The making and giving of cards will give the message that we care. (See also ideas 28, 30 and 35.)

Painting mugs and plates

This activity may take a little longer but provides the children with their own personally decorated mug or plate. A great activity for a workshop approach to your programme.

What you need: A plain mug or plate for each child.
Ceramic paint; small paintbrushes; paper and pencils.
Aprons for the children and coverings for the tables.

What you do:

- Make a template by rolling paper round the mug to measure for size, or place plate on paper and draw round the outside of the plate.
- Cut out template.

- The children then draw their design on the paper.
- When they are happy with their design, use small paintbrushes to paint this onto their mug or plate. The whole mug or plate does not have to be covered in paint.
- Leave to dry for twenty-four hours. During this time, any errors can be corrected by using wet cotton buds.
- Cook in the oven by following the instructions on the pot of ceramic paint.
- The design is now permanent and the mug or plate can be used as desired.

Bible link

The overflowing cup (Psalm 23:5); the cup of cold water (Matthew 10:42).

Using the idea

The designs used will show our creativity. Talk about how God made the earth and everything in it and how he made us like himself – we too can make things.

If a Christian symbol has been chosen, this can be explained, eg fish as a sign used in the early church. Alternatively tie in with a story from the Bible featuring a cup.

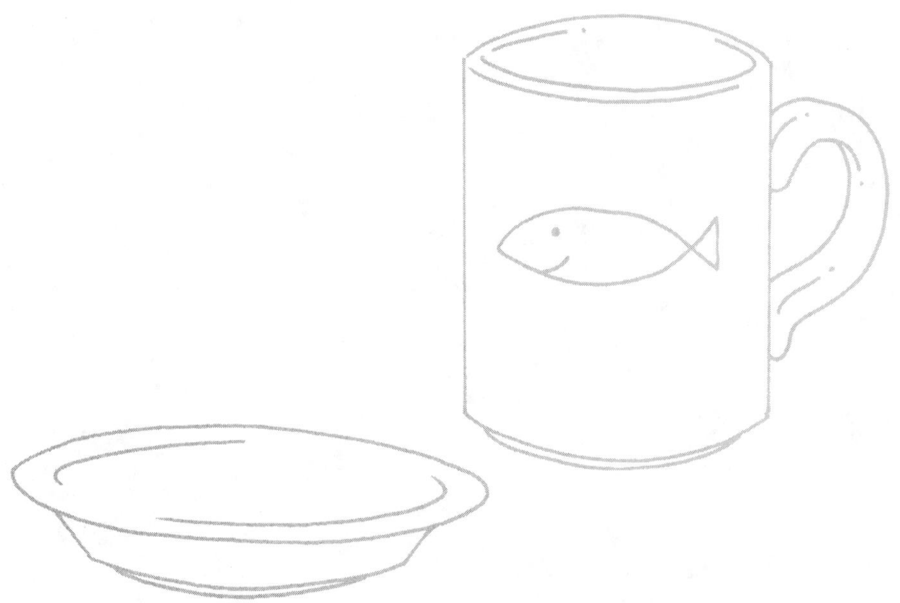

Section Three: **Food Activities**

Food activities are always popular. As they say, 'The way to a man's heart is through his stomach.' I've noticed that it's the same for children! Food activities can be used as opening activities as well as later in the session time. To keep the pace going you will need additional adult help for supervising the washing of hands, baking (if needed), cleaning and tidying of tables and washing up.

Please remember that some children suffer from food allergies. You will need to check before offering food and drink of any kind. This can be done on the application form. Often parents can suggest alternatives so that the activity can go ahead with their child participating. But if any child is allergic to nuts, then that activity cannot take place.

For all food activities surfaces must be clean. We always wipe with anti-bacterial spray and provide a greaseproof paper work mat for each child. The children must wash their hands before beginning, and should not eat food while they are making it.

Unless you are preparing the food to eat during the session, you may prefer the children to take it home. Suitable bags can be provided for this purpose.

Marshmallow pigs

What you need: One large round marshmallow and two small marshmallows per child; Coloured icing pens.

What you do:

- Wash hands and cover table with a sheet of greaseproof paper for each child.
- Use icing pens to stick one small marshmallow onto the centre of the large marshmallow to be the pig's nose.
- Cut the other small marshmallow in half diagonally to be the ears.
- Stick the ears on using the icing pens.
- Use the icing pens to draw on the pig's mouth and eyes.
- The marshmallow pig is now ready to take home and eat.

Bible link

The Prodigal Son (Luke 15:11-31).

Using the idea

Use the marshmallow pigs as a focus for the telling of the story of the Bright-eyed Pigs. The story might go something like this:

Down on the farm a new litter of pigs had just been born. The farmer was really proud of them. They were really bright-eyed and clean-looking. He wanted to keep them that way so he hired a down-and-out to look after them. This young man had been used to life in the city. He had left his dad's farm, taking with him his inheritance for a new life – a better life, or so he thought. That life had been good for a while but then he ran out of money and he realised that all his new-found friends were not really his friends after all. They only wanted what they could get. His only hope of a meal was to take this job.

The Bright-eyed Pigs were pleased to see him as they were after a meal too. This younger son of the farmer back home was good at feeding them. But what about him? He still didn't seem to get enough to eat and he had even thought of eating the pigs' food. But pig's food doesn't look or smell very appetising.

One night he was so hungry he couldn't sleep and he began to think of his old dad and the farm he had left. Even the hired men there had more than enough to eat. 'That's the answer,' he thought. 'I'll go home and offer to be a hired worker. I'm no longer fit to be called my father's son.' So he said goodbye to the pigs and started off home.

There was his old dad on the road looking out for him. He practised what he would say. When his dad saw him he ran to meet him and as he tried to get the words out his dad wouldn't listen. He was more interested in ordering a cloak to be put round him, a ring to be put on his finger and a party to be made ready. He was busy telling everyone, 'This son of mine was lost and now he is found.'

Being the younger son, he had an older brother like younger sons do. This older brother heard all the music and dancing as he was coming in from the fields. 'What's all this about?' he asked. When he heard about his brother coming home he was not too pleased. He was jealous because no parties like this had been thrown for him. His dad tried to explain that he would always have his older son and everything he had was his. He did appreciate him, but he had to celebrate his brother's homecoming because he really thought he would never see him again.

This story tells us how much God loves us. He will let us go away, just like the father in this story let his younger son go, but when we come back, he is so glad.

This idea could be linked to idea 15. The children could make animal masks to wear as you tell the story dramatically.

For younger children, use the marshmallow pigs to help them to remember the story by saying, 'What a shame – all the pigs missed the story. They were so tired that they fell asleep. Now they have woken up, can you tell them the story?' The children then tell their pigs the story.

Making Sweets

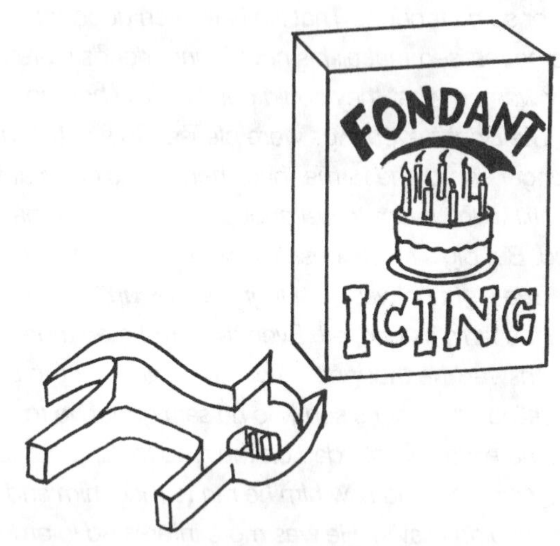

Most children find it hard to resist sweets so a sweet making activity is on course for being a success. This idea suggests two ways of making sweets although, of course, there are many more. They both use fondant icing which can be bought ready made for ease of use.

What you need: Fondant icing – enough for children taking part.
Icing sugar for dusting work mat.
Work mat (piece of greaseproof paper).
Rolling pin and animal-shaped cutters if required.
Food colouring (optional).

What you do:

- Children wash hands and put aprons on.
- Give each child a piece of greaseproof paper to act as a work mat.
- Sprinkle the work mat with icing sugar.
- Give each child a piece of fondant icing.
- The children mould the icing into the shape of their chosen animals.

Alternatively, roll the icing out and cut out shapes with cutters. If desired, a few drops of food colouring can be added to each child's piece of fondant icing.

Bible link

The following are given as examples: the feeding of the five thousand (Matthew 14:14–21); Noah's Ark (Genesis 6:19–22); the story of Creation (Genesis 1); the lost sheep (Luke 15:3–7); the miraculous catch of fish (Luke 5:1–11); Jonah and the whale (Jonah 1:17).

Using the idea

As the children model their animals or cut out the shapes, the story could be told.

The sweets can be used as presents for such occasions as Mothering Sunday or Valentine's Day. Talk about showing our love and care for those close to us and how good it is to give them a gift from time to time to show our appreciation. The children could also make cards to give alongside their gifts.

For younger children, tell the story from an animal's point of view, and afterwards the children can tell the story to the animal. This is a good way to help younger children remember the story.

Making jelly ponds

Jelly ponds are fun to make and eat. They can make a good 3-D model of your chosen Bible story.

What you need: Green jelly made up and left to set in shallow dishes – one for each child.
Coloured fondant icing.

What you do:

- Children wash hands and put on aprons.
- Give each child small pieces of different coloured fondant icing and a jelly pond.
- Children mould the icing into shapes: fishes, frogs, bugs, lilies, baby Moses' basket or bulrushes.

- When moulded, place the icing shapes on the jelly pond.
- The jelly pond is ready to eat.

Bible link

The miraculous catch of fish (Luke 5:1–11); Moses in the bulrushes (Exodus 2:1–10); the plagues in Egypt (Exodus 8).

Using the idea

Before you eat them, use the jelly ponds as a focus for telling the story. Alternatively, tell the story first as a stimulus for making the jelly ponds and then use them to review the story.

Icing biscuits and buns

This is a quick and easy activity which the children really enjoy doing – and eating! It lends itself to celebrations and parties, to sharing and to giving to others to say 'thank you for all you do for me'.

What you need: A biscuit or bun for each child.
Icing sugar mixed to a spreading consistency.
Cake decorations.
Knives for spreading.
Greaseproof paper as work mat for each child.
Paper bags if children are taking them home. (Paper bags can be bought from a Cash-and-Carry or, by arrangement, from a local newsagent.)

What you do:

- Children put aprons on and wash hands.
- Give each child a piece of greaseproof paper as their work mat.
- Give each child their biscuit or bun.
- Share out the icing and the decorations between the children. (Small fromage frais pots are useful for this.)
- Children decorate their biscuit or bun.
- Leave to set.
- If taking home, write each child's name on their paper bag, and place biscuits in the paper bag when set.

Bible link

The wedding at Cana (John 2); the finding of the lost sheep, lost coin and lost son (Luke 15).

Using the idea

Have a party! Party games could be played at the beginning and at the end of the session to set the party atmosphere. Talk about parties and choose one of the party stories from the Bible. The biscuits or buns can be eaten after the story when drinks could also be served. (See also ideas 34, 38 and 41.)

If the children ice more than one biscuit they could keep one for themselves and give the other to someone not at the club. Talk with the children about sharing.

The children could ice a biscuit to give to a member of their family to say 'thank you'. The children could write a card to give with the biscuit. (See also ideas 10, 25 and 28.)

Making edible jewellery

Another activity which children love!

What you need: A packet of Cheerios (or similar) breakfast cereal.
Bowls.
Liquorice laces.

What you do:

- Children wash their hands.
- Give each child a lace and some Cheerios in a bowl.
- Make a knot in one end of the lace.
- Thread the Cheerios onto the laces.
- Tie the ends together.

Using the idea

Why not have a missionary link? Show jewellery or pictures of jewellery made in South and Central America. Talk about the making of it and the selling of it. One project called the Toy Box Charity sells Guatemalan-made jewellery to raise money for its work among the street children in Guatemala. They have rescued many children from the streets and these children now live in homes run by the charity. They are in touch with other children through community projects, including a school, and part of their work is also to keep families together.

Details of the charity, including newsletters especially for children, can be obtained from Toybox Charity. (See also idea 24.)

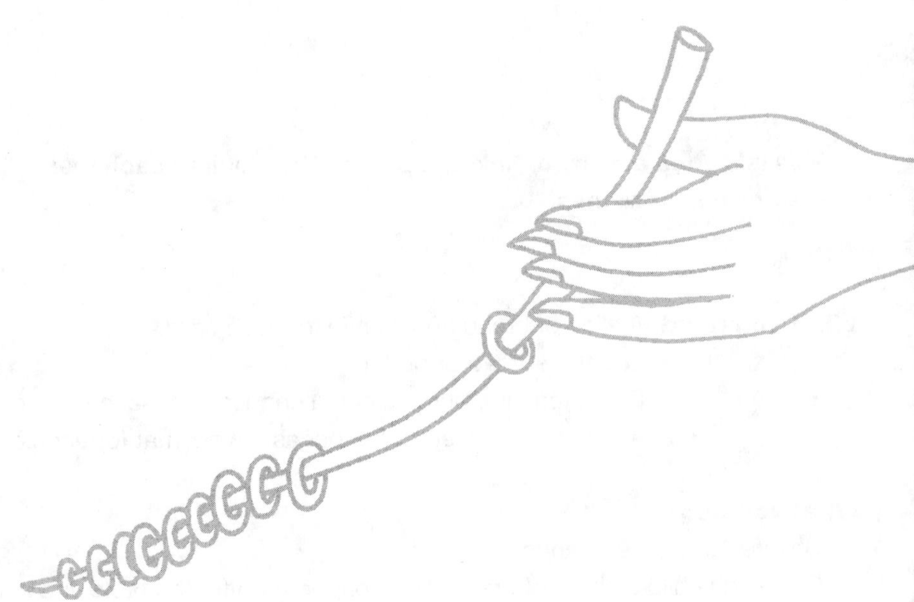

Making sandwiches

This is a good activity to link to a picnic. The children each make their own sandwiches.

What you need: A slice of bread and a knife for each child.
Low-fat spread or butter.
Filling (eg jam, but you could choose cheese, ham, etc).
A sheet of greaseproof paper as a work mat for each child.

What you do:

- Children wash their hands.
- Give each child a sheet of greaseproof paper to coffer the table and act as a work mat.
- Give each child a slice of bread and a knife.
- The children spread the butter onto the bread.

- Cut slice in half.
- Add filling to one half.
- Sandwich together the two halves.
- The sandwich is ready to eat.
- Use the greaseproof work mat to wrap up the sandwich.

Bible link
The feeding of the five thousand (John 6:1–13).

Using the idea
Children sit down with sandwich wrapped in greaseproof paper. Encourage them to imagine they are there at the feeding of the five thousand. You could dramatise the story or have one of the children play the part of the boy. Afterwards, the children can have their own picnic by eating their sandwich. They could also be given a drink at this time.

Making fruit salad

This provides an opportunity to look at unusual fruits and where they come from as well as eating a healthy snack. This could also be added to the picnic in idea 32.

What you need: A selection of fruit – apples, melons, mandarins (clementines, satsumas), strawberries, raspberries, grapes, mangoes, etc.

Tinned pineapple in natural juice as the base for the fruit salad.

A dish for each child.

A knife for each child.

A plate or chopping board for each child.

What you do:

- Children wash hands.
- Give each child a plate or chopping board.
- Children choose their fruit from the selection offered.
- Cut up fruit and place in dish. (Show the children how to cut down through fruit onto the plate or board to avoid cut fingers.)
- Add some tinned pineapple in natural juice.
- The fruit salad is now ready to eat.

Bible link

The fruit of the Spirit (Galatians 5:22–23).

Using the idea

Enjoy tasting the different fruits, then liken them to the fruit that Paul speaks about in Galatians 5.

For a missionary link more unusual fruit could be served (eg star fruit, passion fruit) as well as fruit that the children are more familiar with. Talk about the people in the countries the fruits come from and, if appropriate, the work carried out by Christians in those lands.

Making popcorn

Making popcorn is different and proves a good group activity. It uses the senses of hearing, sight, touch, smell and taste. If you have a popcorn making machine all the better – the children can watch the corn popping through the glass casing. But microwaving popcorn comes a close second.

What you need: Microwaveable popcorn and microwave oven.
Dishes or food bags for serving.

What you do:

- Gather children round the microwave.
- Put in bag as instructed.
- Listen out for popping.

- Leave to cool as directed.
- Share out and eat!

Bible link

The manna in the wilderness (Exodus 16:4–5).

Using the idea

No one knows what manna looked and tasted like, but it was probably a bit like popcorn. Tell the story and finish by eating the popcorn. Drinks could also be served at this point and biscuits for those who don't like popcorn.

Popcorn also makes good accompaniment for watching videos. Younger children will enjoy *Veggietales* (© Big Ideas Productions). Older children will like *Prince of Egypt* (© Dream Works International LLC).

Making biscuits

The children enjoy making and then eating their own biscuits. The recipe below handles a bit like play dough, so it is easy to shape.

What you need: A sheet of greaseproof paper for each child to use as a work mat.

Ingredients for biscuit dough:

150g (6oz) self-raising flour
Half a teaspoon of bicarbonate of soda
100g (4oz) sugar
100g (4oz) margarine
1 egg
1 tablespoon warm golden syrup (optional)
Raisins or chocolate drops for decoration (optional)

Flour to sprinkle on work mat.

Biscuit cutters (if required).
Bowl, spoon, cup, fork.
Baking trays, baking parchment, and wire cooling racks.
Aprons and oven gloves.

What you do:

- Pre-heat oven to 180°C/350°F/gas mark 4.
- Children wash hands and put on aprons.
- Let the children share in making the biscuit dough: Mix together the dry ingredients in a bowl. Rub in the margarine. Whisk an egg in a cup. Add the egg and golden syrup (optional) to the mixture. Knead into a soft dough.
- Divide the mixture between the children.
- The children sprinkle the greaseproof paper work mat with flour and continue kneading their piece of dough on their work mat.
- They can divide it into smaller pieces to flatten down on their work mat with their hands and, after flattening down, use biscuit cutters to cut out shapes. Raisins or chocolate drops can be used for eyes or for decoration.
- Place shapes onto a greased baking tray or onto baking parchment.
- An adult should bake these in the oven for about 10 minutes.
- Gently lift the biscuits off the tray and leave to cool on a wire rack.
- Once cool, the biscuits can be eaten.

Bible link

The feeding of the five thousand (John 6:1–13); the finding of the lost sheep, the lost coin and the lost son (Luke 15); Noah's Ark (Genesis 6–8).

Using the idea

The children will want to eat their own biscuits but they could also be encouraged to make one to give to someone else – maybe their mum, dad, brother, sister, etc at home. Talk about sharing or showing our love for someone else by making and giving them a present. Biscuits could be made for Valentine's Day or Mothering Sunday.

Tell the story and use the biscuits to share in the party atmosphere. Drinks could also be served at this time.

Alternatively, use animal cutters to cut out the shapes as a focus for telling the story of Noah's Ark. The children could cut out two of every animal.

Making bread rolls

Bread rolls smell wonderful as they are baking and taste great warm from the oven. Fillings could be provided if you wish.

What you need: Bread mix or pizza base mix made up as instructed – enough for each child to make one roll.

Flour.

Greaseproof paper, baking trays, cooling trays, and oven gloves.

Paper bags to put the bread rolls in.

What you do:

- Children wash and dry their hands.
- Pre-heat the oven as directed on the packet of your chosen mix.
- Give each child a piece of greaseproof paper as their personal work space.

- Children knead the dough and shape into roll. The roll could be plaited or made into a letter of the alphabet.
- Place the rolls on a baking tray, each on its own piece of named baking parchment.
- Bake in the oven following directions on the packet.
- Children wash their hands and then write their name on a paper bag.
- When cooked, lift the rolls off baking tray and, still on named baking parchment, place on cooling rack to cool.
- Children eat or take home in a named paper bag.

Bible link

Feeding the five thousand (John 6:1–13); Elijah and the ravens (1 Kings 17:1–6); Elijah and the widow (1 Kings 17:8–16); manna in the desert (Exodus 16).

Using the idea

Use the bread-making as a focus for your chosen story. Elijah and the widow lends itself to talking about the smell of baking bread as well:

It was time for Elijah to move on from the brook. God had used ravens to bring him meat and bread for breakfast and supper but now, as there had been no rain for a long time, the brook had dried up and God was moving him on. God took him to the home of a woman in a place called Zarephath.

When he arrived in Zarephath he found the woman gathering sticks. He asked her for a drink of water – he was thirsty – and also for some bread. The woman told him that she only had a handful of flour and a little oil, enough for the last meal she had planned to eat with her son. She was expecting to die of starvation.

Elijah told her to make the bread. What a wonderful smell! But this was not her last meal. To her surprise, the jar of flour and the jug of oil did not run out until God sent rain.

Making bread without yeast

This tastes different from the bread we usually eat, but the children we have made it with find it very 'more-ish.' The honey sweetens it. It can be served on its own or with spread.

What you need: ***Ingredients for bread dough:***

2 cups of flour
2 tablespoons of margarine
½ cup of water
1½ teaspoons of honey
1 teaspoon of salt
Flat teaspoon of baking powder

A piece of greaseproof paper for each child as a work mat.
Baking tray, baking parchment, and oven gloves.

What you do:

- Pre-heat oven to 180°C/350°F/Gas mark 4.
- Children wash their hands and put on aprons.
- Let the children help to mix the dough: Mix dry ingredients together. Add margarine and rub it in using fingertips to crumble. Add water and honey slowly, mixing with a spoon. Knead together to form a ball.
- Divide the dough between the children.
- Children continue to knead their bread on their greaseproof paper work mat.
- They can pat dough down with hands, or use a rolling pin, until it is flat.
- Place on a lightly greased baking sheet.
- An adult should bake these for approximately 10 minutes.
- Leave to cool.

Bible link

The Last Supper (Mark 14:12–26).

Using the idea

Tell the story of Jesus' last supper with his disciples. When you reach the part in the story when Jesus broke the bread, you could share the bread the children have made. Or you could finish the story and then go back to that part of the story again, sharing the bread and possibly having a drink at that time too.

You may want to explain why Jesus and his friends were remembering the Passover and why they used unleavened bread (see Exodus 12).

Making pizza

Children like making their own pizzas. They can put on their favourite toppings. The pizzas look good and taste good too!

What you need: A small pizza base for each child or a larger one between a group of children.

Tomato paste or tomato sauce, or cheese sauce if preferred.

Toppings (eg grated cheese, ham, tomatoes, mushrooms, pineapple pieces).

Knives.

Baking trays.

Oven gloves and aprons.

What you do:

- Pre-heat oven to 200°C/400°F/Gas mark 6.
- Children wash their hands and put on aprons.
- Give each child or group of children a pizza base.
- Children spread pizza base with tomato paste or sauce.
- Provide a selection of toppings for children to choose from.
- Children place toppings on pizza.
- An adult places the pizzas directly on oven shelf for 10 minutes.

Bible link

Paul in Rome (Acts 28:11–16).

Using the idea

Pizzas are Italian. As you eat your pizzas, talk about Paul, who went to Rome. He was put in prison, though, and spent his time writing to encourage all the churches he had established. Those letters are available for us to read too.

Growing cress heads

Some children like looking after seeds, watering them and watching them grow. The seeds should have grown into cress plants after about a week. They can then enjoy eating the cress in sandwiches.

What you need: Cress seeds.
A washed egg shell for each child.
Egg boxes to stand the shells in.
Moist cotton wool.
Felt pens.

What you do:

- Give each child an egg shell to decorate with a face using felt pens.
- Place a small piece of moist cotton wool inside the shell.

- Sprinkle a small number of cress seeds onto the cotton wool.
- Place in egg boxes on the windowsill and watch them grow!
- Water as required to keep moist.
- Eat in sandwiches.

Bible link

Parable of the sower (Matthew 13:1–9).

Using the idea

Seeds will only grow in the right conditions. Having told the story of the sower you may want to tell the children that this type of story is called a parable. A parable is a story with a meaning. The meaning of this story is explained in Matthew 13:18–23. The story could also be dramatised.

Section Four: **Energetic Games**

Children are full of energy, and an active game near the beginning of your session may help to use up some of that energy. The following games are designed with that in mind, but if you want to make a Bible link these are included – albeit tenuous in some cases.

Relay races

These are quick and easy to organise and there are many variations, depending on the equipment available. These are games for when all the children have arrived. The game is first explained in general terms and then an example is given for using it to link in with the Bible teaching.

1. Relay races in general

What you need: Masking tape.
Props for your chosen game.

What you do:

- Divide the children into equal teams, or use the teams the children are already grouped in. If teams are not equal, one child in each team with lower numbers will need to run twice.
- Mark the start and return lines with masking tape.

- Sit children in teams behind the starting line.
- Explain your chosen race idea:
  - Run carrying a plastic beaker / bean bag / ball to the return line and back.
  - Run balancing a bean bag / cup on head to the return line and back.
  - Bounce a ball to the return line, run back with it.
  - Dribble a ball with feet / with uni-hockey sticks / by bouncing to the return line and back.
  - Place two buckets / chairs / hoops between start and return lines. Children run round / bounce or dribble ball round obstacles.
  - Skip to return line and back.
- Each player must wait until the one in front of them has given them the ball / bean bag / skipping rope, etc.
- The winning team is the one with everyone sitting with their arms folded in their line. Award points to the team and to the members of the team as fits your scheme.

2. Example of a Bible link – feeding the pigs (Luke 15:14–16)

What you need: Masking tape.
Three containers for each group – these could be buckets, bowls or boxes.
Bean bags or small balls.

What you do:

- Children stand in a line behind the start line with a container.
- Another container, holding the ‘pods’, is opposite each team on the return line.
- The first child holds the team’s bucket.
- On the command ‘Go’, the first child in each team runs to collect a ‘pod’, puts it in their bucket and runs back to their team where they tip the ‘pod’ into the ‘feeding trough’ and give the bucket to the next player.
- They join the back of the team and the game continues until all the ‘pods’ have been tipped into the ‘feeding trough’.
- The winning team is the one sitting down first with all their ‘pods’ in the ‘feeding trough’.

Bible link

The Prodigal Son (Luke 15:11–32).

Using the idea

Use the game to introduce the story or to highlight a part of it – for example when the Prodigal Son is down on his luck and has to take a job feeding the pigs. Life isn't going to plan. What does he do? Luke tells us that 'he came to his senses'. He didn't stay there with a dead-end job and a hungry feeling in his tummy. He came to his senses. He remembered his former life, he made a decision and he went back home. It wasn't easy, because he had left for a 'better life'. He had to eat 'humble pie' and admit that he had made the wrong choice. We all want to feel that we are in the right but he made his decision.

This story is a parable so you may want to explain to the children that parables are stories with meanings and go on to look at the meaning of this story, making the application to our own lives. This can be done in different ways but one way is to say that it's never too late to turn our lives round. We may not have made the best choices but we can always go back to an earlier place where things were better. With older children who may be a bit 'off the rails' and rebellious, this could mean co-operating a bit more at home or school.

God is like the father in this story – waiting for his son to come home. God is waiting for us too. When we choose to get to know God better, he is so pleased that he throws a party for us in heaven.

Should you wish to link the games and activities for the whole session to this story, ideas 15 and 27 could also be included in your programme.

Bun relay

This game has an obvious food connection and could be linked with a food activity like icing buns.

What you need: Masking tape or hoops to mark out 'plates'.
Beanbags.

What you do:

- Mark two plate shapes on the floor with the masking tape (or use a hoop) – one at each end of the room for each team.
- Divide the children into teams. Each team needs a runner and the rest of the team are the 'buns'.
- The runner starts at one end, the 'buns' at the other.

- The runner carries the 'cherry' (beanbag) and runs to collect a 'bun' from the 'plate' at other end of room.
- Together they run back, with the 'bun' trying to balance the 'cherry' on their head, to the 'home plate'.
- The runner leaves the 'bun' on the 'plate', takes the 'cherry' and returns for the next 'bun'.
- This continues until all the 'buns' are on the 'home plate'.
- If teams are not too big, the race can be repeated with new runners.

Bible link
Herod's birthday party (Matthew 14:3–12).

Using the idea
Not all birthday parties go well and this one didn't. People there were scheming and they got their way. Herod's step-daughter danced at the party and she danced so well that he promised to give her anything she asked for. She could have asked for half his kingdom and he would have given it to her but she didn't. She asked for the head of John the Baptist.

Herod had thrown John into prison because John had told him that he had been wrong to leave his wife and marry the wife of Philip, his half brother. His new wife was called Herodias and she didn't like John. She wanted him killed and this was her moment. When her daughter asked her what she should ask for, Herodias told her to say, 'The head of John the Baptist on a dish.' She did what her mother said.

Herod knew that John was a good man, but he was afraid to go back on his word in front of all his guests so he sent a guard to the prison and had John's head cut off. This pleased Herodias. I'm not sure what it did for her daughter except that she would know she had pleased her mother, but it left Herod feeling very sad.

What about us? Do we follow the crowd even when we know that what they are doing is wrong? Or do we stand up for what we believe to be right? Are we courageous enough to speak up for someone who is being bullied by others? Or do we join in with the bullying?

For younger children you could tell one of the party stories in the Bible.

Bangers and mash

Quick and easy to organise, this is fast-moving and uses up lots of energy. The name of the game can be changed to one of your choosing (eg Spiders and Flies; the names of local towns; names of countries; types of animals). Or use words that fit with your Bible teaching for the session.

What you need: A room large enough for the children to run from one side to the other.

What you do:

- One wall is 'Bangers' and the other is 'Mash'.
- Children start by standing in the middle of the room.
- The leader chooses whether to call out 'Bangers' or 'Mash'.

- The children run and touch the appropriate wall.
- The call can be given mid-run to add confusion.
- The last runner to reach the wall is out and joins the leader to watch for 'last runners'.

Bible link

The Exodus (Exodus 5–14).

Using the idea

Play the game substituting 'Egypt' for 'Bangers' and 'the Promised Land' for 'Mash'.

Talk about not knowing where you are in this game, and this is just how it was for the Israelites when God was leading them out of Egypt. Pharaoh just kept changing his mind. He would say 'yes' and then he would say 'no'. Eventually the Israelites left, but even then he changed his mind and sent his army after them. (See also ideas 2, 14 and 37.)

Have you got it?

A great favourite with our children and asked for week after week. We try to keep it for suitable occasions.

What you need: Objects placed around the room (eg saucepan, book, brush, picture frame, boot).
A table or chair to put the items on.

What you do:

- Divide children into equal sized teams and appoint (or they choose) a runner.
- Place a table or chair in the middle of the room.
- Leader calls out an item.
- The first runner to bring that item to the table or chair wins the point.

- The leader can also call out items that the children might have with them (eg watch, hairslide, shoe, jumper).
- Winning team is the one with the most points.

Bible link

The escape from Egypt (Exodus 12:33–36).

Using the idea

Use the game as a focus for this story from Exodus. The Egyptians were urging the Israelites to leave quickly. So they gathered up their dough before they had had time to add the yeast, but before they left, they asked the Egyptians for articles of silver, gold and items of clothing. This the Egyptians willingly gave. (See also idea 37.)

Shoes and pans

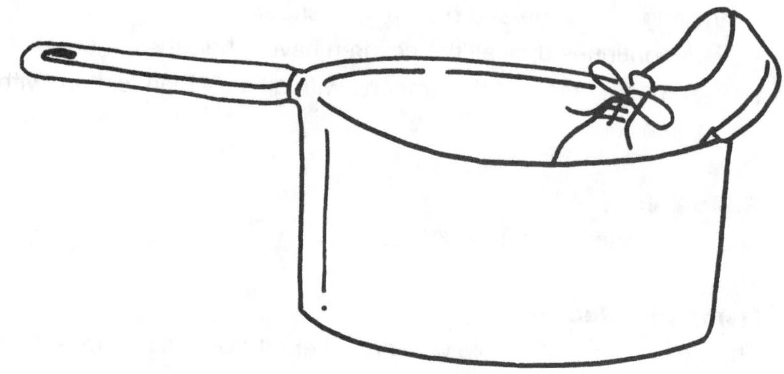

We devised this game to support the teaching of the Veggietales video *Who Is My Neighbour?* (© Big Ideas Productions Inc.). If you don't have the video, the game can be played for fun.

What you need: Children's shoes (as their shoes may not be named, we've found it best for the children to remove only one shoe so, at the end, they are wearing one to match up with!).
A medium or large saucepan for each team.
Masking tape to mark lines.

What you do:

- Divide children into equal teams.
- Each team is in their own corner of the room.

- The children each take off one shoe and place it in a pile in the middle of the room.
- Children sit in a line, one behind the other, behind a marked line on the floor.
- The first child in each team is given a pan.
- On the word 'Go' the first child in each team runs to the pile of shoes and finds their own shoe, puts it in the pan and runs to their team. As they cross the line, they tip their shoe out of the pan, give their pan to the next child, join the end of the line and put on their shoe.
- This continues until all the children have found their shoes.
- The winning team is the first one with all their team sitting, with their shoes on, in a line.

Bible link

The Good Samaritan (Luke 10:25–37).

Using the idea

The video is about people who are different from us and tells the story of the folk in one town who wear pots on their heads and those in another town who wear shoes on their heads. They don't like each other – a little bit like the Jews and the Samaritans in the Bible story of the Good Samaritan. It is the one from the other town who helps the person who has been hurt – not, as you would expect, one of his own townspeople. In this story, the excuse is that they are too busy.

This game could either be played before watching the video to set the scene, or afterwards for fun. If using before, a painting activity could also be included where the children paint previously cut out large shapes of pans and shoes. The children could be kept waiting for the answer to the question 'What do pans and shoes have in common?' Answer: 'They are worn on heads.'

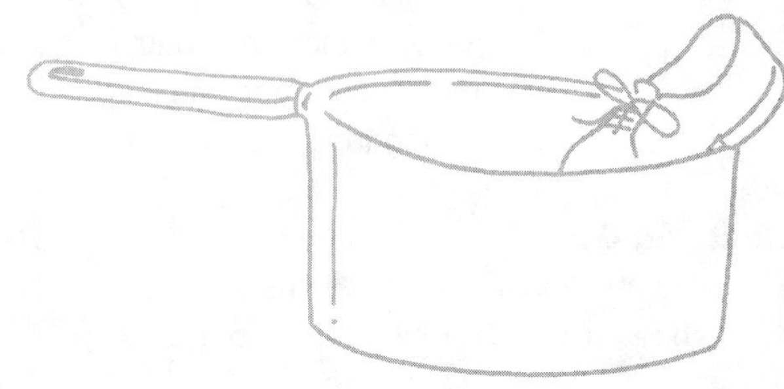

Football, uni-hockey and basketball

Team games are popular with older children who are into sport. They are not popular with the less sporty children. The really keen children like to play a good game – ten minutes each way – where they can really get into the game. They can become very competitive so will need an unbiased referee. Team games are most successful when offered as a choice activity.

What you need: A safe outside play area or a suitably sized room.
Football: ball, goal posts or markers.
Basketball or netball: ball and posts.
Uni-hockey: sticks, ball and posts.
Bibs or bands to distinguish teams (optional).

What you do:

- Divide the children into equal teams.
- If you have more than two teams, run this like a tournament and keep it fast-moving by the quick turn-around of teams.
- Local rules apply – these you will make to best suit the venue and numbers of children.

Bible link

The body of Christ (1 Corinthians 12:14–20).

Using the idea

Use the game to talk about working as a team. If our goalie tries to score the goals, who will stop the ball going in our net? If a striker spends all his or her time in defence who will score? (This can be made relevant to the game you have just been playing.) The responsibilities of the different positions in the game all help the team to be more successful. When we do our part, even if it isn't the position that gets all the limelight, we are laying down our own glory for the better glory of the team. We are working together – that's teamwork.

It's the same in the club. We all have our own place in the club. We don't need to try to do what someone else does or be someone we are not. We can work together for the good of the club, just like the players do in the game and we can do that by respecting each other, and treating each other as we would like to be treated. We all need to feel valued, accepted by the others and that we belong.

You may want to conclude by saying that this is how God made us to be. (See also idea 58.)

Obstacle course

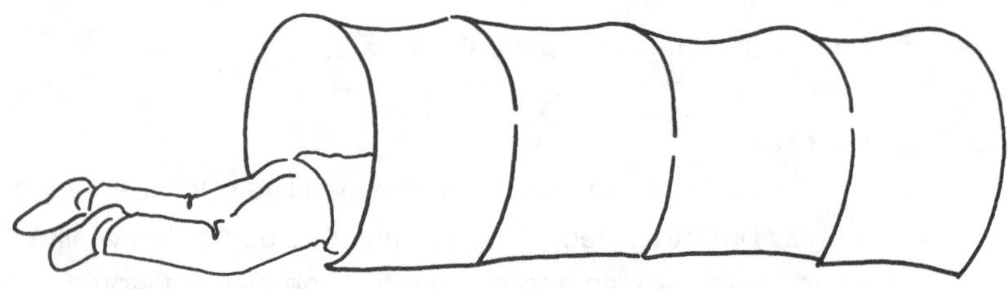

Obstacle courses are always fun and can be made with whatever equipment you have available.

What you need: Masking tape to mark starting line.
Obstacles as suggested below.

What you do:

- Set out an obstacle course using what you have to hand, eg
  - table to crawl under
  - hoop to jump in / stand in and pull up over head / bounce a ball in
  - skipping ropes
  - ball to bounce / dribble
  - bean bag to balance on head

- chairs / buckets / cones to weave in and out of
- net / parachute to crawl under
- play tunnels to crawl through

- Divide the children into teams.
- Mark the starting line.
- Explain, and have demonstrated, what the children have to do.
- Have a practice race.
- Race for real.

Bible link

Living the Christian life (Ephesians 4:25—5:2).

Using the idea

The game could be used to talk about how we live our lives. We may want to do things one way but other people try to influence us not to live like that. Their influence can be the obstacle to our living in the way we would choose.

Most of us know what is right and wrong. Do we live in the way we know to be right, or do we join with others in doing the things that we know are wrong? What are some of these wrong ways of living? (Lying, cheating, stealing, bullying, [drinking, smoking].) If we are tempted to do these things, we will overcome the obstacle when we say 'no' to doing them.

For children who are wanting to live for Jesus, it will not be easy. Obstacles come our way. These may be people who tease us, or the effort of getting up for church, reading our Bible or saying our prayers. How we cope with the obstacles is what matters. Do we give up completely or do we carry on? Reading *Pilgrim's Progress* by John Bunyan may be a spur to keep going. *A Dangerous Journey* by Alan Parry (Candle Publishing) is a good paraphrase to use with children.

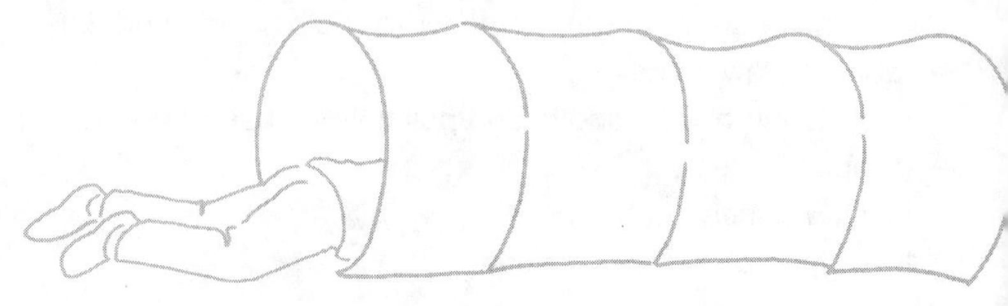

Pass the ball

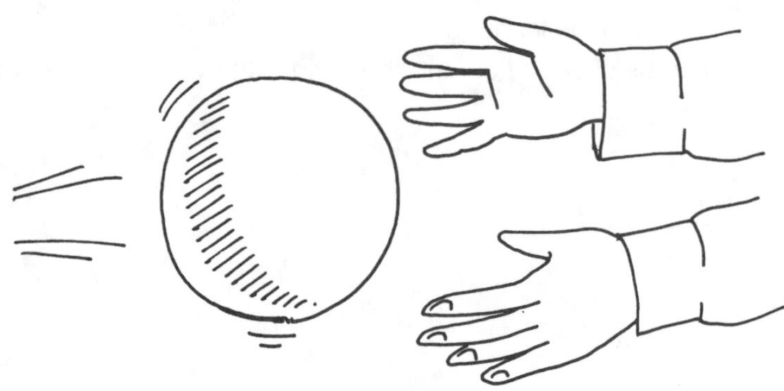

This can be a good opening activity, as children can join in the game as they arrive. It can be as fast-moving as you like and can have an element of competition if desired.

What you need: A ball.

What you do:

- Children stand in a circle.
- Leader passes the ball to a child in a certain way (eg two-handed pass, shoulder pass, bounce pass, between legs, etc).
- Child uses same pass back to leader.
- This can be speeded up and if children drop the ball, they could be given a forfeit (eg stand on one leg, kneel down, catch with one hand, etc).

Using the idea

This game can be used as a fun and active way of learning a verse from the Bible.

- Play the game but don't penalise the children for dropping the ball.
- When the children are happy with the passing, give each child one word of the Bible verse. They say their word when the ball is passed to them.
- Pass the ball in order round the group so that the verse is heard each time round to help the learning process.
- This can be speeded up and then end with everyone saying the whole verse together.

Stop and go

This game is a listening game for younger children. The children need to listen carefully to the colour called.

What you need: A large enough space.

What you do:

- The leader stands at one end of the room and the children at the other.
- The leader's back is to the children.
- The leader counts '1–2–3 green light'. On the words 'green light', the children run towards the leader who continues counting '1–2–3 red light'.
- On 'red light' the children must stop and remain still. If the leader sees any children running, those children have to go back to the starting wall.
- The first child to reach the leader while the lights are on green is the winner.

Using the idea

Traffic lights tell cars when to go and when to stop. Trains also have to obey lights and so too do boats on rivers. The lights tell us when it is safe to 'go' or when it is not safe and we must 'stop'.

If you are talking to the children about prayer, this game could be played as an introduction to how God answers our prayers. His answer might be 'yes', the 'green light', we can go. Or sometimes God might say 'no, stop' or 'not just yet'. God has given us the 'red light'.

Cat and mouse

This game works better with older children who can move quickly on command. Fun and energetic once played at speed.

What you need: A large enough space.

What you do:

- Divide the children into equal teams.
- Have them stand in their lines and measure with their arms a space an arm's length to their sides and from front to back. The purpose of this is so that they can touch the hands of the people on either side and in front or behind to form a barrier for the other players.
- Choose a cat and a mouse.
- The children start with their arms out to the side, touching the hands of the children on each side, and the cat and mouse choose their starting positions.

- The cat must try to catch the mouse by running between the lines without breaking through the barrier made by the outstretched arms.
- The leader can change the direction of the lines by calling 'change' and the lines change by turning to the left and making a new line.
- Speeding this up makes life more difficult for the cat and mouse.
- The game is over when the mouse is caught.
- A new cat and mouse can be chosen.

Bible link

The story of Jonah (Jonah 1).

Using the idea

In the game, the mouse is running away from the cat. In our lives, what do we run away from? And why?

A man called Jonah was running away from God. Why? Because he didn't want to do what God wanted him to do. Why? Because he didn't like the people that God wanted him to go to. Jonah knew that if he took God's message to these people they might just do what God was telling them to do and he didn't want them to. He would rather see these people die than see them turn back to God. (See also idea 77.)

Section Five:
Not-So-Energetic Games

These games are not so active and can absorb children as they focus on the activity. Some can be used as opening activities and others lend themselves to a calming time at the end of the session.

Catching bugs / fish

Whenever we have played this game the children have loved it. The aim is to collect as many Smarties as you can – this is obviously the main attraction. The children also like the challenge of the catching and the idea of the Smarties representing fish or bugs.

What you need: A clean sheet.
A supply of Smarties or similar coloured sweets.
A plastic plate for each team.
A collecting bowl for each team.
A lollipop stick or spoon for each team.

What you do:

- Lay a clean sheet on the floor.
- Spread out your supply of Smarties all over the sheet.
- Divide the children into equal teams of up to five or six.
- Number the children in each team.
- Provide each team with a lollipop stick or spoon, a plastic plate and a collecting bowl.
- The leader calls out a colour, eg red.
- Number one in each team starts by trying to flick red Smarties onto their plate using the lollipop stick or the handle end of a spoon.
- When all the red Smarties have been claimed, the children tip them into their team bowl and pass the plate and lollipop stick to number two.
- The leader calls out the next colour.
- Number two tries to flick the Smarties of that colour onto the plate.
- The game continues until all the children have had their turn and all the Smarties have been 'caught'.
- Count the Smarties in each team's bowl. The winning team is the one with the most.
- The prize is to share the Smarties between the team members.

Bible link

Moses in the bulrushes (Exodus 1—2:10).

Using the idea

Set the scene along the banks of the River Nile. Talk about the river, the fish, the frogs, the bugs around and then talk about the king.

The king was treating the Israelites very cruelly. He had made them his slaves but he was also afraid of them because there were so many of them. He missed the point that because these were God's people God was on their side. He came up with a plan to get rid of some of them. He would have all the baby boys drowned. Not a nice man!

One mother hid her baby boy for three months. Then she had an idea. She would make a basket out of reeds and waterproof it with tar, then put the baby inside and float it on the river among the reeds. She knew that the king's daughter would come down to the river to bathe – they didn't have baths and showers in their houses like we do. She knew that the baby would be found.

When the king's daughter came down to the river, she did find the basket. When she opened the lid she saw the baby and immediately fell in love with him. The princess knew that the baby was an Israelite child but as she didn't have any children of her own, she decided to keep him. She named him Moses.

Continue this story for as long as you choose.

ALTERNATIVE IDEA

You may want the children to think about waiting. We live in a country where we want everything immediately. Sometimes it is better to wait, as this helps us to appreciate what we are wanting. Think about saving up – for a new bike, a computer game, a certain toy.

To give the children an experience of waiting, you could make them wait until the end of the session before sharing out the Smarties. When we did this, we asked the children how they felt about waiting for them. Most children said that they found it really hard – with the exception of the boy who didn't like Smarties!

Guess who / Follow the leader

There are two games in this idea. The objective of the first game is to guess who is causing the children to slide off their chairs and, for the first player, how they are causing it to happen. Subsequent players know the key to the game! This game is best suited to older children who can wink discreetly. If playing with younger children present, they could blink. A popular game.

The second game is similar. This involves following the nominated leader. The child taken out of the room has to work out who the other children are following.

1. Guess who

What you need: A circle of chairs, one for each child.

What you do:

- The children sit in a circle.
- One child is taken out of the room while the leader nominates a child to wink or, for younger children, blink.
- When the child returns, the nominated child winks at another child in the circle.
- As he or she does so, that child slides off the chair and sits on the floor.
- The child who was taken out of the room tries to work out who is doing the winking.
- When they have guessed correctly, they change places with the winker, who is taken out of the room while a new winker is nominated.

2. Follow the leader

- The nominated child leads the other children in an action, eg tapping foot, nodding head, waving hand.
- The child taken out of the room tries to work out which child is leading the actions.

Bible link

The calling of the disciples (Matthew 4:18–22; John 1:35–42).

Using the idea

Are people who are watching your life able to guess who you are following? Do you follow the crowd? The latest craze? Are you up to date with the latest fashion? Are you a telly addict?

Tell the story of Jesus' first friends. They chose to follow Jesus and everybody knew it because their lives changed. Andrew, Simon Peter, James and John were no longer fishermen. Matthew was no longer cheating people by asking for more money than he should when they paid their taxes.

Finish the story with the challenge 'Who do you follow?' (See also idea 5.)

Do you fit?

Another very popular game. Best with older children.

What you need: Chairs in a semicircle.

What you do:

- The children stand round the semicircle, one in front of each chair.
- One child stands facing them at the front.
- That child thinks of a criterion (eg school attended, colour of shoes, type of trousers, supports a certain football team, colour of hair, wearing anything of a particular colour) and walks round the semicircle saying to each player either, 'Want you' or, 'Don't want you.'
- If the child is wanted they stay standing. If the child is not wanted, they sit down.

- When all the children have been chosen or not chosen, they look at those still standing and try to guess the criterion by which those standing have been chosen.
- The person who guesses correctly first becomes the next person to choose the criterion.
- Should that person have had a turn already, they choose someone who hasn't to take their place.
- The game continues for as long as you want it to.

Bible link

Chosen (John 15:16).

Using the idea

Ask the children, 'Were you "chosen" or "not chosen"?' In the game it doesn't really matter because we know the choice isn't personal. But how is it in life? How does it feel to be 'chosen'? How does it feel to be 'not chosen'? It feels particularly good if we are chosen by the most popular person in the class to be their friend or because we are really good at something we do (eg playing football). It is really good if we respect and look up to the person who has chosen us.

Well, here's some good news. The Creator of the universe has chosen each one of you. Yes, he wants you on his team. What will you say? (See also idea 3.)

'Caw, raven, caw'

The key to this game is staying quiet and not dissolving into giggles. To add variety on future occasions, the game can be played with the animal sounds of your choice, eg 'baa, sheep, baa', 'roar, lion, roar', 'hee-haw, donkey, hee-haw', etc.

What you need: A circle of chairs.

What you do:

- The children sit on chairs in a circle.
- One child is taken from the room while the other children all change places.
- This child is then blindfolded and brought back into the room.
- The child starts in the middle of the circle and walks towards a child sitting in the circle.
- He or she sits on this child's lap and says, 'Caw, raven, caw.'
- The child on the chair 'caws'.

- The child sitting on his or her lap has to guess who it is.
- If he or she guesses correctly, they change places and the game begins again.
- If the guess is wrong, they try another lap until they guess correctly or until they've had a long enough turn.

Bible link

Elijah fed by ravens (1 Kings 17:1–6). For other animal sounds: 'Baa, sheep, baa', the lost sheep (Luke 15:3–7); 'Roar, lion, roar', Daniel in the lions' den (Daniel 6); 'Hee-haw, donkey, hee-haw', Balaam and his donkey (Numbers 22:21–41).

Using the idea

Use the game to introduce your chosen story. For example:

How many of you have had your breakfast brought to you by ravens? There was a man in the Bible called Elijah who was camping down by a stream. He had just told the king, whose name was Ahab, that there would be no rain until God said so. King Ahab wasn't following in God's ways and God was angry with him. Now no rain would mean no crops, no water. It would mean famine and drought. King Ahab was angry with Elijah and so, after Elijah had given King Ahab this message from God, God told him to go camping. Well, not quite in those words. He told him to hide by a brook in the Kerith Ravine.

It was a nice place, although a bit isolated and not in easy reach of the shops. But soon there would be no food in them anyway – remember no rain means no water, no crops, no food, famine and drought. But God told him not to worry about that. God said, 'You will drink from the brook and I have ordered the ravens to feed you there.' Elijah went, just as God had told him to, and 'the ravens brought him bread and meat in the morning and bread and meat in the evening, and he drank from the brook'. Amazing!

God took care of Elijah during this time of no rain. You may want to continue the story in future weeks by telling the children about when the brook dried up (1 Kings 17:7–16), and what happened three years later when God was ready to send the rain again (1 Kings 18:16–46). Idea 35 (bread making) could be used to illustrate the story of the widow of Zarephath and pictures could be painted or the altar drawn and the flames made by sticking red, yellow and orange tissue paper onto the paper to illustrate the story of Elijah on Mount Carmel. This could also be a group project (see idea 17).

Still lions / Lions' stalk

Lions can be very quiet and still when hunting. The first idea is about lying still – an ideal way to get some peace and quiet after more energetic activities. The second, 'Lions' stalk', is a game rather like musical statues. Choose some slow-moving music and encourage the children to move slowly and carefully round the room. When the music stops they must remain very still. A good game for younger children.

1. Still lions

What you need: A large enough space for all the children to lie down.

What you do:

- Tell the children how quiet and still lions can be when they are hunting.

- The children lie still on the floor.
- The leader (or a nominated child) walks round looking at the 'lions'.
- He or she can try to make them laugh or move but must not touch them.
- When a 'lion' moves, he or she is out.
- The winner is the 'lion' that stays still for the longest.

2. Lions' stalk

What you need: Space.
Music on tape or CD.

What you do:

- As the music plays, the children move round the room slowly, carefully looking from side to side.
- When the music stops, the children stop and keep very still. Tell them that they are waiting to pounce on their prey.
- If they move they are out because the prey will see them and run away so those 'lions' will have lost their dinner.
- When out, the children help you to watch the other lions.

Bible link

Daniel in the lions' den (Daniel 6).

Using the idea

The lions in the Bible story today are hungry. Their tummies are rumbling and they are looking forward to a nice meal. They are in a pit so they won't be stalking like lions in the bush. Will they eat Daniel?

Daniel was a good man who was doing all that God told him. He's in the lions' den because other people have set him up. They tricked the king into making a law, knowing that Daniel would be found to be breaking it because the law prevented people from praying to anyone except the king. They knew that Daniel wouldn't keep this law because, although he liked the king and got on well with him, Daniel prayed to God and nothing would stop him doing that – not even being threatened with being the lions' next meal.

Daniel prays. Even the king prays, because he doesn't want Daniel to be eaten. He likes Daniel. The kings prays, 'May your God, whom you serve continually, rescue you.' The king doesn't sleep too well and the next morning he comes to see if his prayer has been answered.

God was with Daniel and his trust in God caused the king to see that Daniel's God was the true God. Daniel's God answered prayer. So, the king brought out another law. This time all the people were to worship Daniel's God.

(See also idea 15.)

In size order

A quick and easy game to organise. The older children usually take charge.

What you need: No equipment needed.

What you do:

- Divide children into teams.
- Each team stands in a line.
- On the word 'go', the teams must organise themselves into height order.
- The winning team is the first to achieve this.
- For a greater challenge, repeat with eyes closed.

Bible link

David and Goliath (1 Samuel 17).

Using the idea

Who's the tallest? How tall are you? How tall was Goliath? (You could build his height with boxes.) How tall was David? David wasn't the biggest but he was the bravest. He was prepared to fight Goliath because he could see what this was all about. It was really an attack on God. The Israelites were the people of God and David knew that God was on their side. This was about the honour of God's people and, therefore, the honour of God.

David was amazed that no one would fight and, when he offered, King Saul tried to make him do it his way. David was given Saul's armour to wear, but that was far too big and uncomfortable so he quickly took it off. He went as he was, taking his sling with him and picking up some pebbles from the stream as he went. David was an accomplished 'pebble slinger'. He had killed lions and bears with his sling so why not this giant of a man? There was plenty of him to hit and he wouldn't be a fast-moving target.

For older children you could emphasise that David did it his way, using his experience of life and his abilities. What do we do when we face giants in our lives? Who or what will our giants be? They won't be like Goliath but they may make us afraid. (See also idea 56.)

Shoe sizes

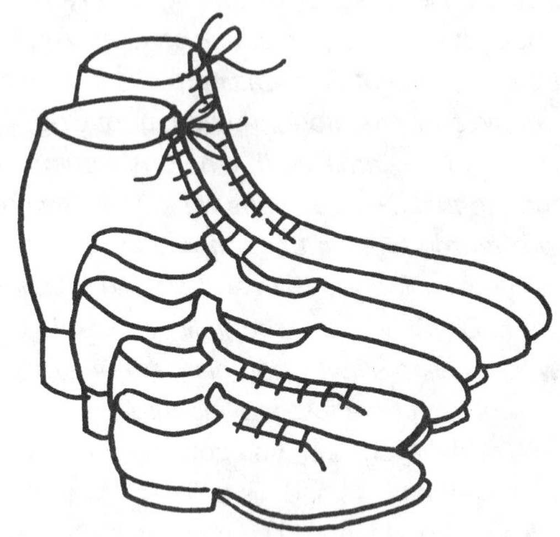

Before starting this game, make sure that the children either have their names in their shoes or know what their shoes look like. Particularly check whether children in the same team have the same style of shoes. You want the children to go home in their own shoes!

What you need: Children's shoes (if named) – or shoe (if not named).

What you do:

- Group the children into teams of mixed ages.
- Children take their shoes off (or just one shoe if you want to be able to match the shoes with the child).
- On the word 'go' the teams must arrange their shoes in size order.

- The winning team is the one with their shoes in the correct order and the team standing in a line behind them.

Bible link

David and Goliath (1 Samuel 17).

Using the idea

The story of David and Goliath is about a man with really big feet. In fact, he had enormous feet – the size of five or six of your feet put together. He didn't just have enormous feet, he had enormous everything. His hands, his arms, his legs … and where was his head? It's way up there. (Look up, shielding eyes.) Tell the story of how David went to fight Goliath to save God's people. The story could be dramatised. (See also idea 55.)

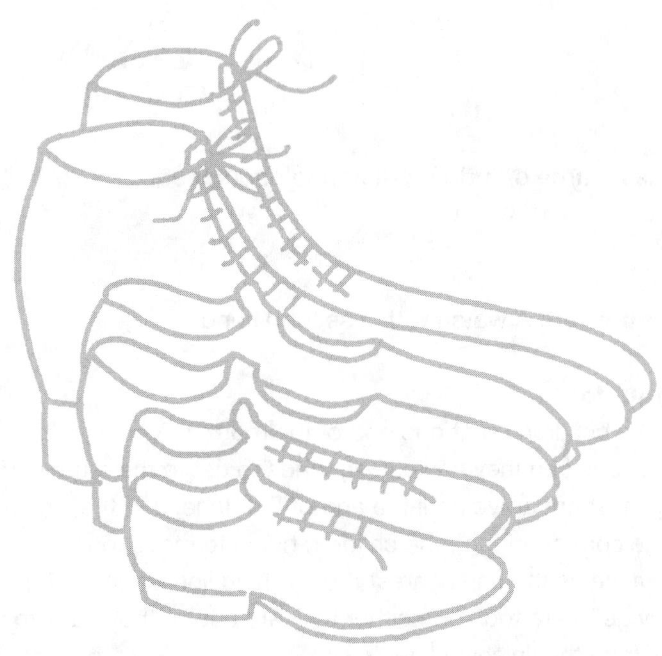

Snail race

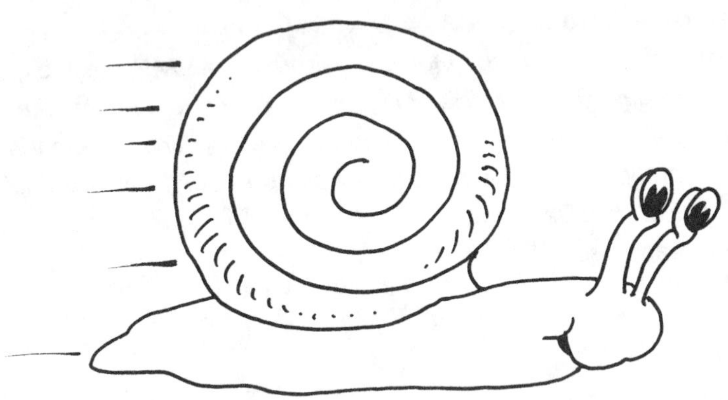

This is a game of judging distance and speed.

What you need: A watch with a second hand.

What you do:

- Line the children up at one end of the room.
- Tell the children they have 30 seconds to get to the other end of the room. They must not arrive until the end of that time, and they must keep moving.
- On the command 'go', the children begin to move towards the finish line.
- The winner is the one nearest the finishing line when the time is up.
- If they get there too soon either they are out, or they have to start moving away from the finishing line.

Bible link

Balaam's donkey (Numbers 22:21– 41).

Using the idea

In the game you were judging speed and distance. A man in the Bible called Balaam had a problem with judging – judging what he should be doing. It resulted in the arrival of an angel. Ever seen one of those? And his donkey talked! Yes, talked. Well, the donkey was as surprised as you. People talk, donkeys hee-haw and that's how it is … but not that day. The donkey could see the angel but Balaam couldn't … and that was the problem. Tell the story of what happened that day on the road to Moab.

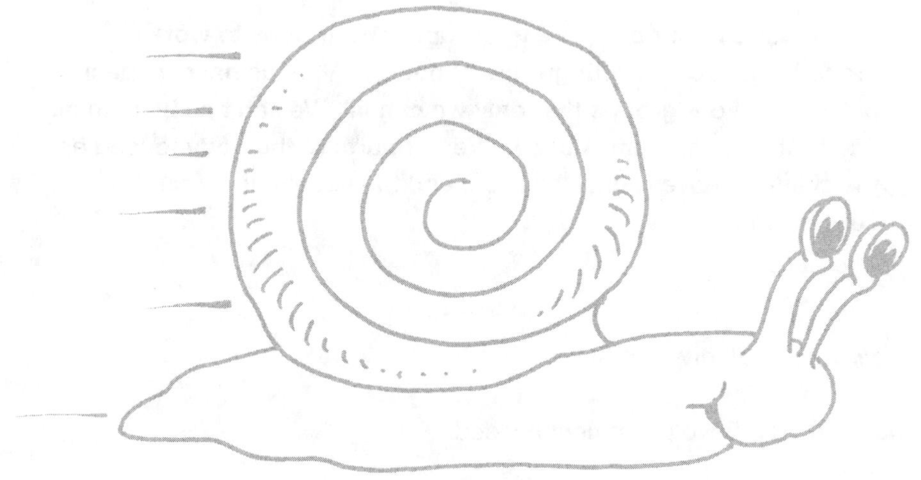

Follow your elbow / Are you a nose?

All the parts of our body are important for our body to work properly and so it is with groups of people. All of us have a special place within our groups that only we can fill. We can't all be a nose. The first of these games uses different parts of the body to lead as the children move round the room and the second is a race to collect sweets.

1. Follow your elbow

What you need: No equipment needed.

What you do:

- Divide the children into teams of three and number them 1, 2 and 3.
- The children stand in a line one behind the other in their teams.

- The child at the front begins as the leader (number 1), calling out a part of their body to lead, eg elbow, nose, ear, knee, back, and setting off round the room.
- The rest of their team follow using the same part of their body to lead.
- From time to time, the team leaders can change the leading body part.
- The team must follow by making the change.
- Change the leader by calling out a number.
- Make sure all have the same opportunity to lead their team.

2. Are you a nose?

This game can be played with sweets shaped as body parts which, at the time of writing, are made by Rowntrees.

What you need: Enough sweets for all children.
One bowl for each team.
Plastic cup or food bag for each child.
Masking tape.

What you do:

- The children stand in a line behind masking tape line on the floor, facing a bowl of body part sweets.
- Each child has a cup or food bag.
- On command 'go', the first child runs to the bowl to collect a sweet, puts it in the cup or food bag, then runs back and joins the end of the line.
- The next child goes as first child crosses the masking tape.
- Continue until all have had a turn.
- The winning team is the first to be standing quietly in their line.
- Gather children together. Look at different sweets. Try to identify shapes (ears, noses, mouths, etc).
- Talk about body parts.
- After the talk, the children can eat the sweets.

Bible link

The body of Christ (1 Corinthians 12:12–31); the parable of the talents (Matthew 25:14–30).

Using the idea

Talk about the different parts of the body and their functions and liken them to the parts we all have to play within our families, class at school and the club. Where do you fit? What are you good at? God has made each of us to fit into our place – no one else can fit there. God has made us for a job that only we can do and no one else can do it. Those who seem to be weaker than us need our help because they are important for the group we are in to work properly – they are as important as those who seem to be strong, the cool guys, the most popular.

Are you a nose? An eye – watching out for the group? A head – the brains of the group? A foot – taking the group forward? A mouth – speaking up for others, speaking out good ideas? A shoulder – for others to cry on and find comfort in? An ear – listening to what others have to say? A hand – to make the squash, to give out the biscuits, to help other people?

Be happy with who you are. Know you have your role and know that we need each other because it is impossible for any one of us to do or to be everything … and it would be lonely anyway. Respect others for who they are and work together where you can.

Help the children to think about the things they are good at and how they can use these gifts (talents) if they are not doing so already. This is an opportunity to build up self-esteem, self-confidence, self-worth.

Maybe, if appropriate, some of these gifts and talents can be used in the group.

(See also idea 45.)

Flap the Fish

There is skill in flapping the fish as, to succeed, air must move underneath the fish to make it move forward.

What you need: A folded newspaper for each team.
A large paper fish cut from paper, about 30cm long, for each team.
Masking tape.

What you do:

- Mark start and finish line on the floor with masking tape.
- Divide the children into teams.
- Have half of each team stand in a line at one end of the room, with the other half standing in a line facing them.

- On the word 'go' the first child starts by flapping the fish with the newspaper to make it travel towards the finish line.
- When it crosses the line at the other end, the newspaper is given to the next player.
- Play continues until all children have taken their turn.
- The winning team is the one that finishes first.

Bible link

Paul all at sea (Acts 27).

Using the idea

Ever been in a storm? Well, imagine it. The wind is blowing hard (children blow), the rain is pouring down (drum by patting two fingers of each hand together), the waves are crashing (clap hands once) and a fish is hiding under the waves. This fish is watching as the ship above tosses this way and that.

The voyage started off OK although it was not a good time of the year to sail. Having been lulled into a sense of security by the gentle wind and thinking that this was just what they needed, they set sail. But then came the wind (blow), the rain (drum) and the crashing (clap) of the waves. It was hurricane force. Ever been in a hurricane? Ever seen what a hurricane can do? Watch the television next time you hear of a hurricane hitting the coast of, quite often, America. It's not a pretty sight. Houses get pushed down, cars blown over, boats in the harbour sink.

The sailors on this ship secured it as best they could although it was hard to even stand up. They had to hold onto ropes to move about on the deck. They threw the cargo overboard to try to lighten the ship. 'Cargo overboard! Watch your heads!' the fish shouted in its loudest fish voice. (Do fish have a voice?)

The men on the ship had gone without food. Now one of the passengers stood up. Well, he wasn't actually a passenger, more a prisoner. He was on his way to trial in Rome. It was fortunate for the others that he was on the ship. He told them not to be afraid because God had told him that they would make it. The sailors hadn't listened to him before when he advised them not to sail. Would they listen now? His name was Paul.

The storm was still tossing the ship about fourteen days later. The wind was blowing (blow), the rain was driving (drum) and the waves were pounding (clap).

But the sailors sensed they were near land. Some of them got this idea of lowering the lifeboat and sneaking off – well, wouldn't you? But Paul found out and the centurion – a special kind of guard looking after Paul – stopped them. Paul said they were to eat. He took some bread and gave thanks to God for it, broke it and began to eat. The others did the same.

Next day they could see the land. They tried to sail the ship towards it but it ran aground. Then the soldiers planned to kill the prisoners to stop them escaping but the centurion wouldn't let them as he didn't want Paul killed. He ordered all those who could swim to swim ashore and those who couldn't ('What! Can't swim?' said the fish!) to find planks of wood to float on. Everyone reached land safely and no one was lost.

Section Six:
Party Games and Challenges

The following party games are included for fun and team building. They can also be used to set the scene for Bible teaching, and Bible links are included should you wish to use them in this way. They can be played simply as party games with the aim of having a good time, or they can be used as group challenges, with a competitive element introduced.

The challenge can be over half a term, with a small number of children taking part each week while the other children cheer them on, or during one session if you prefer. For some of the activities a record can be made of each child's score with the winner being the one scoring the greatest number by the end of the competition. A chart can be made for all the children to watch progress.

For other activities, the winning child goes forward to the next round when they compete again until the winner is found in the finals. At the end a prize could be given to the winner, and maybe the runner-up.

The following have been used by a group in Sheffield which plays them as competitions over a number of weeks – depending on the game. The children all have a lot of fun and really enjoy them.

For each game you will need an egg timer or a watch with a second hand for timing each child's turn. (In Sheffield they use a big egg timer which stands six inches high!)

Pick a pea

This is a competition between two players.

What you need: A straw and two bowls for each child, one containing dried peas. An egg timer or a watch with a second hand.

What you do:

- On the command 'go', the children try to suck a pea onto the end of the straw and keep sucking while they move the pea above the second bowl.
- Stop sucking and let the pea drop into the bowl.
- Keep going until the time is up.
- The winner is the one with the most peas in their second bowl.
- Keep a score to see who transfers the most peas by the end of the competition.

Bible link
The wheat and the weeds (Matthew 13:24–30).

Using the idea
Was it easy to pick up the peas? What about the different grains in your bowl of muesli? Ever tried to separate those by hand? (Could this be another game!) Hard, isn't it? Or what about pulling up weeds in the flower bed. Not easy if the flowers are growing too. Try it – but ask your mum or dad first. They may want to come with you to make sure that the flowers aren't pulled up at the same time. Exactly like the man in this story.

His servants came to tell him about the weeds growing among his wheat and they wanted to pull them up. He said, 'No. Let them grow together and at harvest time we'll ask the harvesters to separate them.'

This story is a parable, a story with a meaning. If you want to know its meaning, you can find it in Matthew 13:36–43. (You may not want to tell the children this part of the story, though.)

Ping-pong race

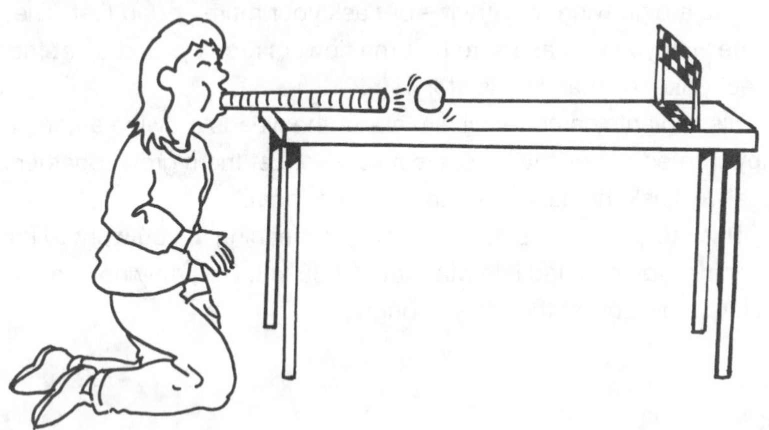

This game is for two players at a time.

What you need: A straw and ping-pong ball for each child.
Masking tape to mark start and finishing line on the floor or table.
An egg timer or a watch with a second hand.

What you do:

- On the command 'go', the children blow through the straw to make the ping-pong ball move across the table.
- The child whose ping-pong ball reaches the finishing line first is the winner.
- That child goes forward to the next round.

- A chart can be kept showing who played whom, and listing the winners of each round.
- The competition ends when the final winner is found.

Bible link

Keep going (1 Corinthians 9:24–25).

Using the idea

It's not always easy to keep the ping-pong ball going in the right direction and sometimes it won't move at all. When the power is in the right place, it can sail along. You could use this as an illustration for the Bible teaching – the key is to keep going.

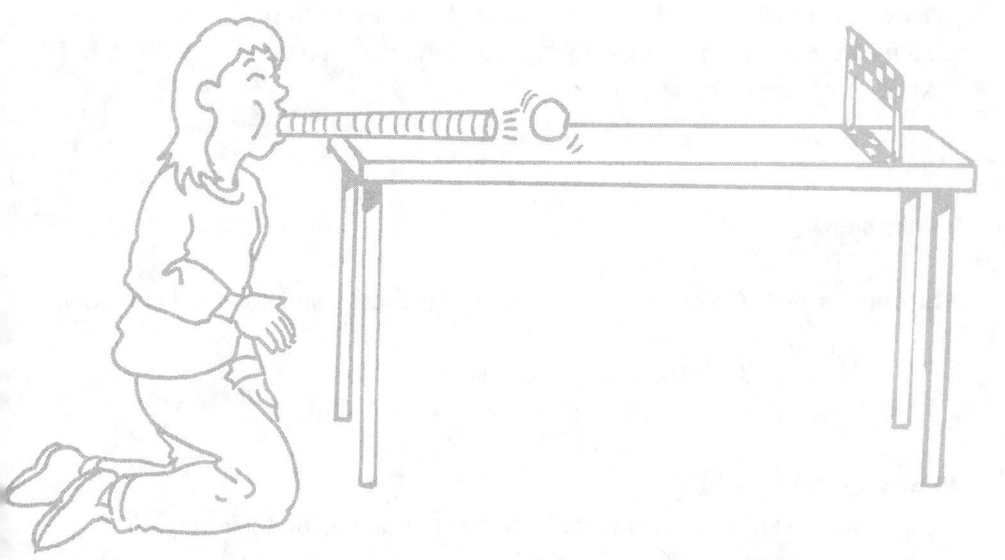

Jelly slurp / Saucer of milk

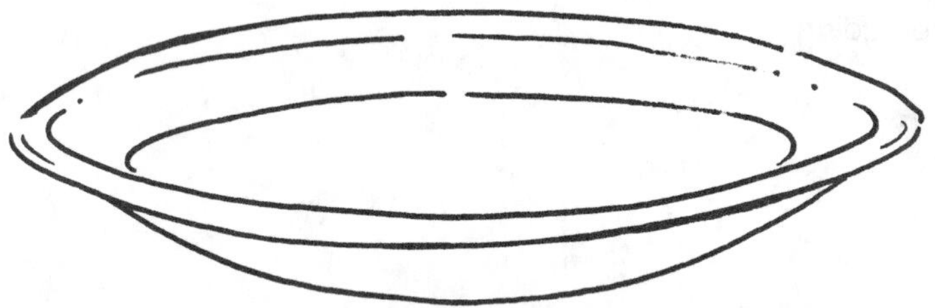

These two games are for four players. They are both played in the same way, with the first being played with jelly on a plate and the second with milk on a saucer.

1. Jelly slurp

What you need: A pint of jelly made up as instructed and spooned onto four plates.
A plastic cover for the floor.
A timer or a watch with a second hand.

What you do:

- The children kneel by their plate with their hands behind their backs. Other children are ready to cheer them on.

- On the command 'go', they suck the jelly off the plate.
- The winner is the child to eat the most jelly in the time allowed.
- That child goes forward to the next round.

2. Saucer of milk

What you need: A saucer of milk for each child.
Plastic covering for the floor.
A timer or a watch with a second hand.

What you do:

- Play as above but with children lapping the milk. (For younger children: pretending to be cats?)

Bible link

Being a fool for God (1 Corinthians 3:18–23).

Using the idea

You may feel a fool slurping jelly off a plate or lapping milk from a saucer, but you join in because it's fun and you're game for a laugh. Some people think that only fools want to know about God and do things his way. What do we say to ourselves about that? We have to decide: do we want to live God's way? If we do, we can expect that others may think we are fools, but we know that we have all the wisdom of God available to us and that has to be better, doesn't it, because he is our Creator?

The one who makes knows more about what he has made and how he made it than the thing he made can know. He also knows more about what he has made and how it works than anyone else does. Who's foolish? Those who listen to the one who made them or those who ridicule him?

Pinning the tail on the donkey

This game requires the children to be blindfolded. Some children, especially younger ones, don't like this, so you might want to play just with eyes closed.

What you need: A blindfold.
A large picture of a donkey.
A separate picture of the donkey's tail, with Blu-tack attached at the root of the tail.

What you do:

- Pin the large picture of the donkey at child height.
- The children take it in turns to be blindfolded and to try and place the tail on the donkey with other children cheering them on.

- Mark each child's spot with a felt pen code (eg give each child a letter of the alphabet).
- The winning child is the one who is closest to where the tail of the donkey should be.

Bible link

Balaam's donkey (Numbers 22:21–41); Mary's donkey (as presumed used for her journey to Bethlehem); Jesus' donkey (Matthew 21:1–11).

Using the idea

You could tell the story through the eyes of the donkey. For example, see idea 23 where the story is told through the eyes of a spider.

Alternatively the game could be played with putting the tail on the sheep, the lion, the camel, etc and telling a story about that animal.

Twister

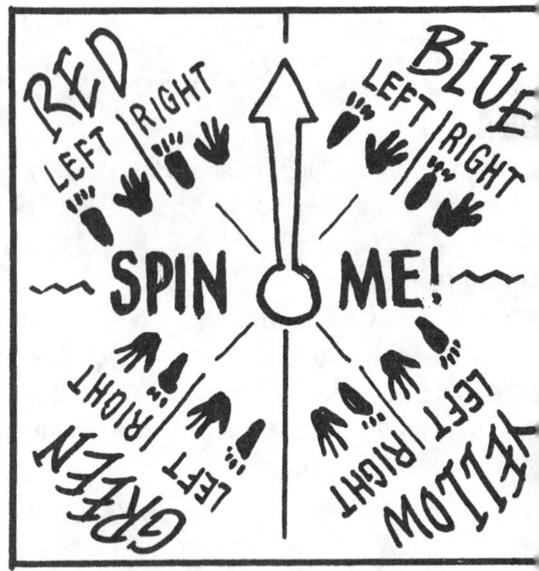

This game is for two or three players at a time and can be purchased in most toy shops. A large floor mat shows different coloured shapes, and players are asked in turn to place a specific hand and foot (left or right) on a specific colour and shape – without falling over. The first player to fall loses.

What you need: A game of Twister.

What you do:

- Play as instructed.
- The winners go forward into the next round.

Bible link

Peter in prison (Acts 12).

Using the idea

Ever been in a difficult situation – not just in a game of Twister but in your life? It happened to Peter. He was arrested and put into prison on a trumped-up charge. It was Passover so Peter had to stay in prison until the festival was over. The church was praying for him.

It was hard for Peter to sleep. He was chained to two soldiers to make doubly sure that he did not escape. However, he was asleep. Suddenly the prison cell was filled with light. Ever seen an angel? Well, here was one. He jabbed Peter in the side to wake him up and told him to get up quickly. Peter got up and the chains fell off his wrists.

The angel told him to put on his clothes and sandals, so he did. Then he told him to put on his cloak and to follow him. Imagine it. He was walking out of prison right in front of the eyes of all the guards who had been put there to keep him in! The best part was going through the prison gates. They just opened for him to pass through. He had walked the length of a street before he realised that the angel had left him, that he wasn't dreaming – this was real – and it left him in no doubt that angels exist. Do you believe in angels?

Now what? He made his way to his friend Mark's mother's house. Her name was Mary. When he knocked at the door, her servant, called Rhoda, answered it. When she heard Peter's voice she was so overjoyed that she forgot to open it. She was running back to tell the others but they thought she was hearing things. The knocking continued and when they opened the door they were amazed to see Peter. All his friends from church were in there. They had stayed to pray and their prayer had been answered.

And what about the guards? Well, they were in a pickle now. Explain that to the king! A search was made for Peter but, as they couldn't find him, the guards were executed.

Feed your partner

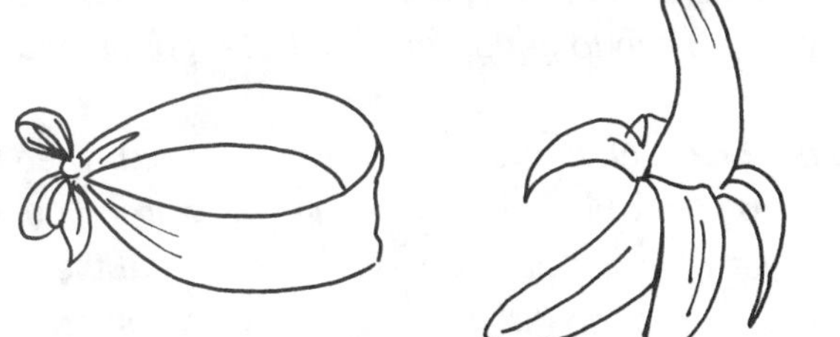

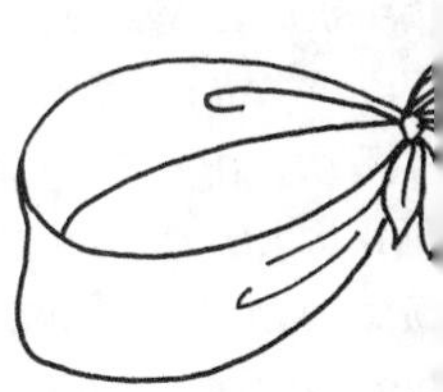

This game is for two players. Check for food allergies before playing.

What you need: A blindfold for each player.
A banana for each player.

What you do:

- Blindfold both players and give each a banana.
- On the command 'go', each player must peel their banana and offer it to the other player.
- The first one to get a bite in the time allowed wins.
- As a reward, the winner gets to eat the rest of the banana they have bitten into.

Bible link

The Passover meal (Exodus 12); in the desert (Exodus 16); Elijah fed by ravens (1 Kings 17:2–6); the widow's meal (1 Kings 17:8–16); the feeding of the five thousand (John 6:1–15).

Using the idea

Talk about being fed and then tell your chosen story of how God fed hungry people in the Bible. (For more suggested stories, see also ideas 53 and 36.)

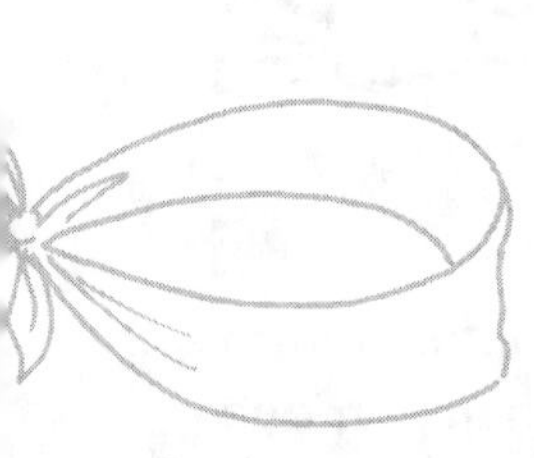

Find the sweet

This game is for four players. Check food allergies before playing. You can use jam, spaghetti or another food rather than porridge if preferred.

What you need: A pint of porridge made up as instructed and divided between four bowls.
Four sweets in each bowl.
A flannel and towel for each child.
A plastic cover for the floor.
A timer or a watch with a second hand.

What you do:

- Children kneel by their bowl, with their hands behind their backs.

- On the command 'go', they try to find the sweets with their mouths.
- The winner is the one who eats their sweets first in the time allowed.

Bible link

The lost sheep, the lost coin, the lost son (Luke 15); the hidden treasure (Matthew 13:44–46).

Using the idea

Talk with the children about how they found the sweet. Then introduce your chosen story. Talk about how the sheep, the coin, the son or the treasure was found. If the game is played over a number of weeks, one of these stories could be told each week.

Catch the apple

This game is for two players.

What you need: Two washing-up bowls.
Two apples.
Plastic cover for floor.
A timer or a watch with a second hand.

What you do:

- Fill the two washing-up bowls with water and float an apple in each one.
- Children kneel by their bowl, hands behind back.
- On the command 'go', they try to catch the apple with their teeth.
- The winner is the first to have hold of the apple in the time allowed.
- Prize – eat the apple!

Bible link

Adam and Eve and the apple (Genesis 3).

Using the idea

When should you not eat an apple? When you are told not to. This is what happened when two people ate the apple they were told not to eat. (Tell the story of Adam and Eve.) The sad thing is they could have eaten the apples on any of the other trees – it was only the apples on this tree that they weren't to eat.

Pinball / Table football

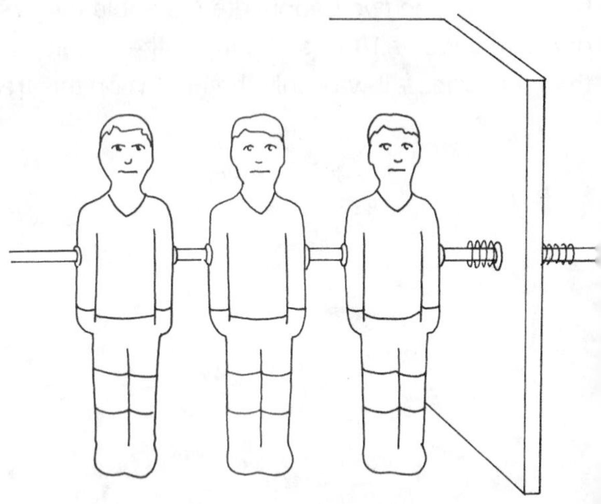

This game is for two players.

What you need: Pinball or table football game.
A timer or a watch with a second hand.

What you do:

- Play the game for a given time.
- Keep each child's score.
- The child with the highest score when everyone has had their turn is the winner.

Bible link

Playing games (Matthew 11:16–17).

Using the idea

Ask questions like, 'What are your favourite games?' 'What do you play most in the playground or with your friends?' 'Do you think Jesus played games when he was a boy? I think he did.'

The Bible tells us that girls and boys liked to play at copying the grown ups – games like 'weddings', 'funerals' or 'soldiers coming into town.' Archaeologists tell us that they played games with dice and had pull-along toys. Joseph was a carpenter so I'm sure he would have made pull-along toys for Jesus when he was little.

Girls used to play with dolls and dolls' houses. Boys would practise with a sling, whirling it around their heads and letting the stone fly to its target. David was very good at this. He practised while looking after his father's sheep and that helped him when he met with Goliath (1 Samuel 17:34–37). Athletics was popular and so was the playing of musical instruments.

And I'm sure that children played at throwing and catching and football.

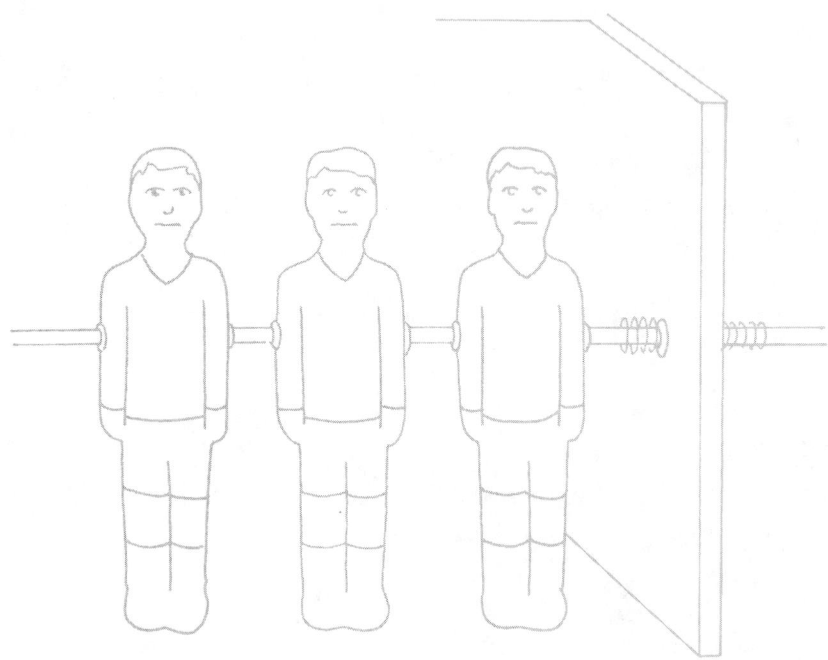

Section Seven: **Telling Stories**

Story time can be much loved if the stories are told in a gripping way. This can be done through the charisma of the storyteller, using voices and actions, and through the participation of the children, with the use of puppets, drama, dance, games, quizzes. To our surprise, even having the stories read directly from the Scriptures enthralled the non-church children in our group. Using videos occasionally can also make an attention-grabbing presentation. Choose ones that are not too long or just use clips from them.

The ideas that follow are intended as tasters to get you presenting stories creatively. Books in the Resources section (page 332) will also give further ideas to inspire you. An area not covered in this book is using illusion to tell stories. This is really attention grabbing but something I have not done. If you would like to explore this further, get in touch with Tricks for Truth.

Dramatised story 1. You the storyteller

The children will be focused on you as you dramatise the story. This is achieved through the way you tell the story, your actions, facial expressions and the clothes you are wearing or the props that you introduce. The children can also be encouraged to participate by using actions, eg rubbing their tummies, or by repeating words. Another approach is to present the story 'pantomime style': 'Oh no he didn't!' 'Oh yes he did!'

What you need: Time to read through your chosen story and jot down some notes to help you.

A selection of props to highlight elements of the story (eg, for the wedding at Cana, flowers, wine glass, hat, etc).

What you do:
Tell your chosen story as dramatically as possible. Don't be afraid to over-act, to shout, or to make large actions. Look through the following story as one possible idea.

Bible link
The wedding at Cana (John 2).

Using the idea
Ever been to a wedding? Well, this was a wedding and a half!

A friend of Jesus' family was getting married. All the village had been invited and the place was full of people.

If you've ever been to a wedding, you know how people enjoy eating (rub your tummy and say 'yum') and drinking (say, 'Come on, let's drink!'). Get children joining in with an echo response like: *OK eat (children echo eat), drink (drink), eat (eat), drink (drink), eat (eat), drink (drink), eat (eat) … Oh no! There's no drink left!*

This is awful. What are we going to do?

Jesus' mum goes to find him. Then she says to the men in charge of the drinks, 'Do what he tells you.' Jesus is in a corner here – should he do what his mum says? He does.

He looks round and sees the water jars. They are there because it's sandy and people wear sandals, and the sand gets between your toes, and after walking to someone's house your feet need a wash – no cars or buses, you see. Anyway, Jesus sees the water jars and he asks the men to fill them with – yes, you've guessed it – water. Then he says to the men, 'Taste it.' What a joke! But it's not.

Wow! The water tastes like the best wine! When the guests drink it they say, 'Hey man, why did you keep the best wine until last?'

Well, the men who filled the jars knew the answer to that, didn't they? And so do we. What Jesus did in changing the water into wine is called a miracle and this was Jesus' first miracle.

Dramatised story 2. Using words and actions

Before the story is told, the children are given words to listen out for with corresponding actions to perform. This encourages them to listen and to be involved in the telling of the story.

What you need: Time to read the story beforehand and to rewrite it in a way that is true to the story, but which includes certain words. See the example below for ideas.

What you do:

- Divide the children into groups or teams.
- Give each group a word to listen out for and an action or a sound to go with the word.

- Tell the story.
- When they hear their word, they must do the action or make the sound.

Bible link
The story of the lost sheep (Luke 15:1–7).

Using the idea
Tell the children the words or sounds that you want them to listen out for and do the actions or make the sounds.

Possible words:
Sheep: on all fours, say baaa.
Shepherd: stand up, hand shields eyes, look around.
Lost: stand up, bend down and look through legs.
Hillside: stand and join fingertips above head.

A **shepherd** had 100 **sheep**. Every day he took the **sheep** out onto the **hillside** to feed. Every night the **shepherd** counted them back off the **hillside** into the pen. He was pleased that not one was **lost**. One day, when he counted his **sheep** back off the **hillside**, there was one missing. 'Oh, no! I've **lost** a **sheep** out on the **hillside**!' the **shepherd** exclaimed. The **shepherd** made sure that the other **sheep** who were not **lost** were safe in their pen and he went out to look for his **lost sheep.**

The **shepherd** climbed onto the **hillside** to look for his **lost sheep**. The **shepherd** looked for his **lost sheep** on the **hillside** behind bushes, behind trees, behind rocks. The **shepherd** finally found his **lost sheep** on a ledge on the **hillside**. The **shepherd** picked up his **lost sheep** and carried it off the **hillside** back home to join the other **sheep**, which were not **lost**, in the pen. The **shepherd** then invited his friends to a party because he was so happy that his **sheep** that was **lost** on the **hillside** was now found and not **lost** any more.

An active story

This idea is similar to idea 70 in that the children have to listen out for key words. This time, instead of doing actions when they hear their word, they run round the circle back to their place.

What you need: A circle of chairs or a parachute.

What you do:

- The children sit in a circle, on chairs or around a parachute.
- Give the children a key name or number from the story. Two or three children round the circle have the same name or number.
- Tell or retell the story. Each time the key name or number is used, those children run round the circle, all in the same direction, and back to their place.

Bible link

This can be used with any Bible story. Try it out with the story in idea 70.

Using puppets

It is amazing how children respond to puppets. Many are caught up with the illusion that the puppets are real. They are amused by them, but will also listen to them and dialogue with them. Puppets can be used in different ways to tell the story – you might even have a go at ventriloquism!

You can do the story yourself, or use a puppet team for such presentations. This can be made up of leaders or of children who have previously rehearsed the story a number of times.

What you need: Puppets.
CD or tape player. Suitable CDs or tapes (see Resource section).

What you do:

- Sit the children down and insist on quiet.
- Introduce your puppet(s) and say who they are.
- Begin the story, using the puppets to create dialogue or argument, or to underline your chosen point.
- Finish by thanking the puppets for coming, and letting the children wave goodbye to them.

Puppet dialogue

In my opinion, this method is a great help to the less experienced puppeteer. We successfully use a dog in a box to tell younger children about street children. We also regularly use a *Bug's Life* character to tell the story. The puppet was significant to the children as it was called 'Bugz' after the name of the club and, in many ways, represented the club in the eyes of the children.

Puppets can be bought with legs which allow them to sit on your knee, or to sit close to you on a table. Bugz sat in the crook of my arm which brought his mouth to just about the height of my ear!

You can either use a different voice for the puppet, or you repeat what the puppet whispers in your ear – rather like Matthew Corbett used to do with Sooty.

The following example uses the story of Daniel in the lions' den (Daniel 6).

Leader: Who would you like to tell us about today?
Puppet: Daniel.
Leader: What about Daniel?
Puppet: He was in trouble.
Leader: What kind of trouble?
Puppet: There were lions round his feet.
Leader: Lions? What happened?
Puppet: They were hungry and should have eaten him, but they didn't.
Leader: Why not?
Puppet: God stopped them.
Leader: When did God get involved?
Puppet: Well, he was involved from the beginning. Daniel was God's man. He talked to God at the set prayer times. He did only the things God wanted him to do.
Leader: So why was he with the lions?
Puppet: Some men were jealous. They tricked the king into thinking he was a god and making a rule that everyone was to pray to him and to no other god. If they disobeyed they would be tea for the lions. This was a problem for Daniel.
Leader: I see… because Daniel prayed to God.
Puppet: Yes, and the bad men knew this. They waited for him to pray again and then told the king.
Leader: I remember. The king was sad because he liked Daniel but he had to carry out the punishment. So Daniel was with the lions.
Puppet: But he wasn't being eaten.
Leader: So Daniel wasn't in trouble any more. God kept him safe.

(See also ideas 15, 53 and 54.)

Using puppets in story review

This has always worked well for us. The children have looked forward to impressing the puppets with their answers. Following are two ideas. The first has the puppet watching the children. (Who would dare misbehave with the puppet watching them?) The second uses the puppet as a cheer leader for their team. For the second idea, the children work the puppet – a further attraction.

1. Puppet watches children

What you need: Puppet.

What you do:

- Tell the story.
- Use the puppet to watch the children as they listen.

- The puppet asks the questions at the end of the story. To keep the pace fast-moving this can be organised in teams with the answers being given as true/false or, in smaller groups where the pace can slow a little, the children can answer the puppets. Younger children in particular can dialogue with the puppets as if they are real.

2. Puppet as cheer leader

This works well for us with the children working marionette-style puppets, and it appeals to all age groups, although it is better with older children as they have more control over the working of the puppets. The puppets are not expensive and they are easy to use. Each group has its own, which they name, and a different child from the team is chosen to work the puppet each week.

What you need: Puppet, group mascot and bucket for each team.

What you do:

- Each team has a puppet as cheer leader and a team mascot.
- Ask questions with yes/no or true/false answers.
- Put first question to number one in team.
- Number one runs to the bucket and places mascot either on top of the bucket for true/yes or in the bucket for false/no.
- Team cheer leader puppets jump up and down if correct.
- The winning team is the one with the most correct answers.

Bible link

The lost son (Luke 15:11–31).

Using the idea

Tell the story and use the puppets to help the children to remember it. Then ask questions based on the story (bold italics below indicate correct answer):

1. There was once a man and he had ten sons.
   True / ***False***

2. The younger son wanted to go and see the world.
   True / False

3. He asked his dad for his share of the money.
   True / False

4. He went to (name your town).
   True / ***False***

5. He spent loads of money having a good time.
   True / False

6. One day his pockets were empty.
   True / False

7. His friends wouldn't give him any money so he got a job as a dustman.
   True / ***False***

8. He was so hungry, he decided to go to Spain.
   True / ***False***

9. His dad was so pleased to see him, he gave a party.
   True / False

Telling a story using colours

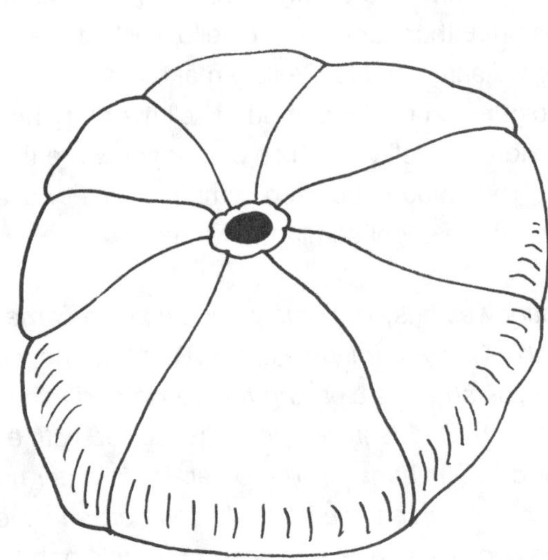

In this idea colours provide a focus for the story. The colours are used symbolically and can be shown by using paper, card, fabric or, if you have one, a colourful parachute. This idea looks at two examples: 'The life of Jesus' and 'The Christian life'. If you are buying a parachute, you could consider colours that can be used for storytelling. The colours of our parachute were chosen with telling the story of Jesus in mind as well as being used for parachute games.

What you need: Coloured squares of paper, card, fabric or a parachute.

What you do:

- Use coloured squares of paper, card, fabric or a parachute to highlight parts of your story.
- Hold up the colour, or look at the colour on the parachute, as you tell the story.

Using the idea

1. The life of Jesus

The children are sitting around the parachute. There are different ways you can begin. Either: 'Look at the yellow. What does yellow make you think of? The sun / light / summer, etc? Yellow makes me think of …' (tell the story). Or 'Which colour am I thinking about?' Tell the story and, when you have finished, ask the children to tell you which colour you were thinking about.

The colours are used symbolically. For example, yellow can be used to think about the angel coming to Mary.

Mary was busy at home when an angel came to tell her that she was to have a baby. Can you imagine that? We don't know exactly what she was doing but maybe she was cleaning the house and thinking about her engagement to Joseph. Suddenly the house was filled with a brightness she had never seen before. The angel spoke to her. He told her not to be afraid – well, you would be afraid, wouldn't you? Angels don't drop in every day! Then he told her that she was going to have a baby and that this baby would be God's son.

Yellow could also be used to talk about Jesus going back to be with his Father in heaven. You could, therefore, return to this colour at the end of the story.

Continue the story, working through the colours in your pile or round the colours on the parachute. This could be done in one sitting or you could choose to talk about a different colour each week as part of a longer project. The teaching focus for the week would be based on a Bible link with that colour. For example, the teaching focus for the week using the idea above could be 'Mary's going to have a baby' or it could be 'Are angels real? They were for Mary'.

The colours below can be used to symbolise the following:

Turquoise: Jesus' baptism.
White: the coming of the Holy Spirit upon Jesus.
Green: Jesus' life and ministry.
Red: Jesus dying on the cross for us.
Black: our sin.
Purple: victory over death, and kingship.
Yellow: returning to the Father / ascension / coming glory.

2. The Christian life

This can be told in a similar way, with the colours being used as follows:

Turquoise: our baptism
White: the coming of the Holy Spirit to us.
Green: our ministry.
Red: asking forgiveness for our sin.
Black: Jesus taking our sin.
Purple: living in the victory Jesus has won for us.

(See also ideas 3 and 76.)

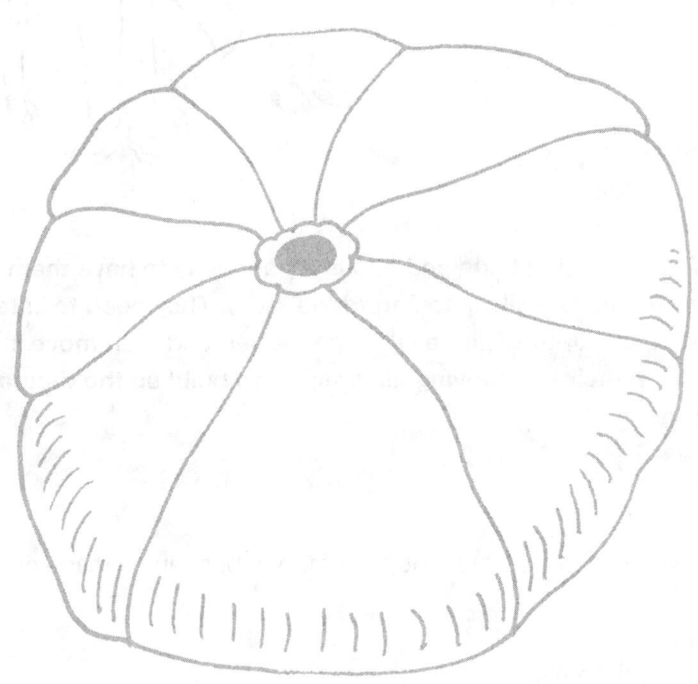

Telling a Story using Flags

Children love using flags and this is a good way to have them actively involved while listening to the story. They need to listen out for the colour of their flag as it is mentioned and then move into the scene with their flag moving as directed to build up the drama of the story.

What you need: Flags (best made out of fabric but can be made out of paper).

What you do:

- Give each child a flag.
- Talk about safety. Remember that flags take up a lot of space, so have everyone spread out as required. Remind the children to watch the flags all the time.

- Teach the children how to use the flags:
  - Try moving flags in a figure of eight in front of body.
  - Walk around with flags dropping behind body (in the example below this is useful for chorus time).
  - Lower the flags gently to the ground (in the example below this is useful for red and green flags).

Using the idea

The following suggests ways of using flags with the song *'Colours of salvation'* (© 1997 Thankyou Music) by Jim Bailey from the CD *Colours of Salvation* (Children's Ministry).

Verse 1: Gold and yellow flags enter dance area either by following round in a circle (flags held behind body), or by dancing and turning with flag in dance area, moving flags in a figure of eight. At the end of the verse, stop in a semicircle with flags held high, as in 'trooping the colour'.

Verse 2: Black flag enters dance area and runs around gold and yellow flags. Gold and yellow flags can lower with point touching ground. At the end of the verse, the black flag leaves the dance area and collects the cross ready for the final chorus.

Verse 3: Red flags enter and float over lowered flags. After the red flags have passed over the lowered flags, the gold and yellow flags lift up while the red flags continue round in a circle in front of the gold and yellow, and point upwards.

Verse 4: White flags enter from each side of the dance area and, with dancers facing each other, move flags in a figure of eight.

Chorus: All colours mix, returning to above finishing positions at end of chorus.

Verse 5: Green flags enter from each side and move around dance area keeping flags 'floating' close to the ground. At the end of the verse, finish in front of the white flags, kneeling down with flags close to ground.

Verse 6: Blue flags enter from each side and fly high over dance area.

Chorus: All colours mix together. This time bring on cross from the rear of the dance area to the centre of the flags. Lift cross high while flags carefully lower to point towards the cross.

(See also ideas 3 and 75.)

Telling a story using a parachute

A parachute, a large piece of muslin or a king-size bed sheet can be used as a prop or visual aid in the telling of many stories. This idea looks at using a parachute to tell three different stories in story review.

What you need: A parachute or a king-size bed sheet, or a large piece of muslin. Muslin is quite inexpensive and can be bought in any fabric shop. It comes in a natural (cream) colour (cheapest) or white and can be dyed to any colour you want.

1. The storm on the lake (Matthew 14:22–33)

What you do:

While telling the story of the storm on the lake, use the parachute in the following ways.

- As the sea – the children create wave-like movements, progressing to the great billows of a storm as the story unfolds.
- As a boat in which the children sail on the sea.
- When the disciples see Jesus walking on the water this can be enacted by holding the parachute taut and having a child walk on it. If enough adults are present, it may be possible to lift the parachute and child off the ground – not so advisable with the muslin or bed sheet as the fabric may not be strong enough to hold the weight of a child!
- This can be repeated with Peter walking on the water. As he does so, gently lower the parachute and as the story proceeds, bring in the giant waves and the storm.
- As Peter calls to Jesus for help, the storm calms and Jesus joins Peter on the lowered parachute and they walk off together.
- Move the parachute gently to denote the calm sea.

2. Other lake stories

- The parachute can be used as the lake in the story of Jesus talking to the crowds (Luke 5:1–3), or calling his disciples (Luke 5:4–11).
- Boxes can be placed on the parachute to represent boats.
- The story can be enacted with the children being the disciples in the boats or the crowd on the shore.

3. Jonah

In the story of Jonah, the parachute, muslin or bed sheet can represent the sea and then the belly of the big fish.

- Begin by moving the parachute gently and, as the story unfolds, make the movements stronger as the storm develops.
- If your parachute has a hole in the middle, Jonah and a sailor or two can be swaying about as if in the boat. (Ensure that large cushions are placed directly beneath the hole in the centre of the parachute.)
- For the time Jonah is asleep, he could be below decks, under the parachute.

- At the point in the story when the sailors throw Jonah overboard, if using a parachute with a hole in it, Jonah could roll onto the parachute and, if the hole is big enough, slip through it.
- All the children could then join him inside the big fish by mushrooming the parachute and moving under it to sit inside. (This may not be so easy with a sheet so the children can stand round the sheet holding it over Jonah.)
- Jonah can sit in the middle making suitable dramatic responses to the story as it continues.
- When Jonah is spat out by the fish, he can move out from one side of the parachute.
- If under a parachute, the other children come out and the parachute becomes the calm sea. (If holding a sheet, the children remain where they are and gently move it.)
- You can continue telling the rest of the story of Jonah while the children are sitting around the parachute.

4. Story review

The parachute is also good for story review requiring careful listening and action.

- The children stand round the parachute.
- Give each child a word in the story to listen out for.
- When the children hear the word, they run under the parachute and out the other side. (See also idea 8.)
- Alternatively, the children can run round the parachute as described in idea 71.

Telling a story using hidden objects

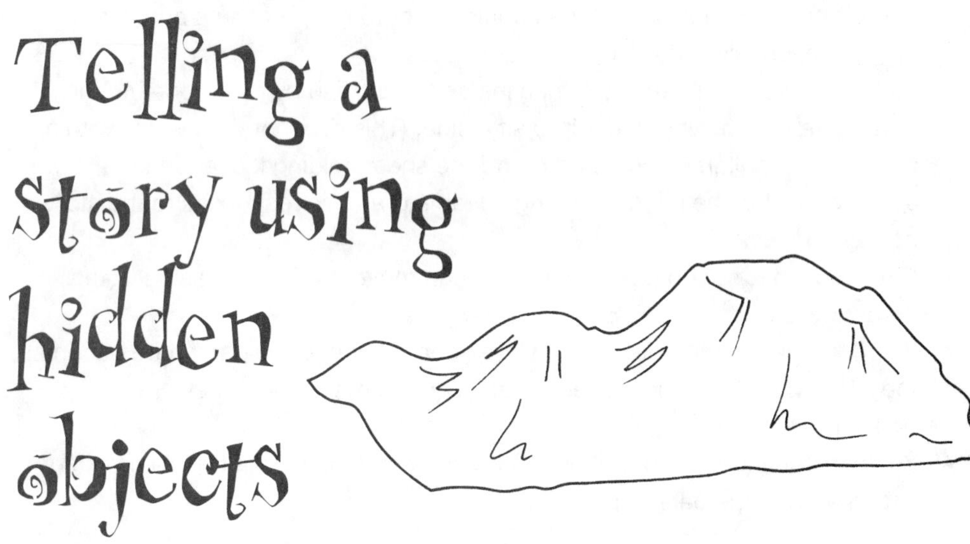

Objects can be hidden in a box or under a parachute if you have one. More suited to younger children.

What you need: A box or a parachute.
A selection of objects suitable for your chosen story.

What you do:

- The children take it in turns to put their hand in the box or to go under the parachute to find an object.
- When all have had their turn talk to the children about things lost and found.

Bible link

The lost coin (Luke 15:8–10).

Using the idea

After playing the game, sit the children round the parachute and ask them, 'Have you ever lost anything? How did you feel? Did you find it? How did that make you feel?'

Tell the story of the lady who lost her coin. The children can help you by following your actions as you tell it… dramatically! For example:

This is the story of a lady who lost a coin. She looked everywhere – under the carpet, behind the sofa, on top of the cupboard (do the actions). She got out her broom and brushed around the skirting boards. She kept looking and brushing until she found it. And how did she feel? What joy! She held a party to celebrate.

(See the story in idea 18.)

Telling stories using dance drama

This idea takes the story of Moses and Pharaoh as an example and develops it through dance drama. A creative way for the children to participate in the telling of the story.

What you need: A tape or CD of your chosen story told in song. (We used *RPM Volume One* CD, available from One Way UK.)

What you do:

- Tell the story of Moses and Pharaoh (Exodus 7–12).
- Listen to the chorus on CD or tape.
- Divide the children into groups of at least four or five or use the teams they are already in if these are not too big. You will need a Moses character for the verses.

Each group works out what they will do during the chorus. This needs to be repetitive, so that it is easy to remember, and quick to slip in between the verses. Allow the children to develop the movements for themselves, but if they need some help, here are some ideas.

1. Moses character with most children either making bricks or building with bricks. Some children could make, while others shape and pass on to those who build.
2. Moses before Pharaoh with the other children being the courtiers. Moses is asking for the release of God's people. Pharaoh is refusing.
3. If wanting to present this to parents or to include in church at a special service, different groups could take different parts of the story. The work can be going on outside the palace while Moses and Pharaoh are meeting.

Between each verse, return to the chorus motif.

Verse 1:
Children become the burning bush. Suggest the children think about how flames move, what colours they are. Ask them how they think Moses would have reacted. Surprised? Frightened? Maybe he would have taken a step backwards or fallen to his knees.

Children have used ribbons / crêpe paper streamers / scarves to be the flames on the bush.

Moses has mimed the taking off of his shoes, has stood in awe or fallen to the ground in response to the voice of the Lord.

Verse 2:
Children enact the people passing through the Red Sea. Moses does what the Lord tells him to do, interpreting the words of the song.

We've had children create the Red Sea by standing facing each other with arms held horizontally and fingertips touching. As the waters part, the children lift their hands. One 12-year-old girl organised the children in her group who were to be the sea into a line. She had the other children weave in and out. We've also had children use blue fabric for the sea. The fabric has been lowered as the people pass across it.

Verse 3:
Children take the part of the army being drowned by the waters. Children I have worked with have really enjoyed interpreting the dying army! They step into the river and, as they walk, the waters return at Moses' command. At this point, the children start to do their dying act, ending up on the floor in different shapes.

Blue fabric could be used for the covering by the waters – the children being the Egyptian army lie under the water.

Using the idea
It is possible to work out a whole group presentation. Ideas need to be explored in smaller groups then shared. Not all the children need participate in every scene and some may change from one to another. For example, children being the burning bush can become the Egyptian army if there aren't quite enough children.

After each verse, the chorus is repeated and the children return to their original motif.

Our main use of this form of storytelling has been in one session, quite quickly – it can be done in 20 minutes. If preparing for a public presentation you will need much longer. You may want to give the children the choice. In this way, you will not be making children do something they don't want to do and those who do want to will enjoy spending more time with it.

Dance drama could be one of your workshop choices. For example, children can choose between dance drama and games.

(See also ideas 90 and 91.)

Reading Stories

Christian bookshops carry a wide range of children's Bibles and story books. It came as a surprise to us when one of our leaders chose to read a story to the children, that they listened so attentively. I wouldn't suggest this approach every week but it can add variety to the presentation of the story time. Some stories are written from a fresh perspective, for example *God's Story* by Karyn Henley (Kingsway), which is written like a continuous story with short chapters, telling the Bible narrative chronologically and true to the text. Books by Bob Hartman like *Bible Baddies* (Lion Publishing) and *Angels, Angels all Around* (Lion Publishing) tell the story imaginatively and from fresh angles.

A story can also be read from a more conventional Bible, too, and the *Lion Children's Bible* (Lion Publishing) has been a popular one with our group.

What you need: A children's Bible or book of Bible stories.

What you do:

- Read with expression and with the expectation that the children will be attentive.
- Make sure that the children are comfortable and not too close together.
- Start positively, with presence and purpose.
- Gain eye contact with the children as often as possible.
- If you can, use different voices for the different characters.
- Facial expression can also help captivate the children.
- Have other adults sitting with the children (these may also be team leaders). This will help to keep the children focused on the story. Or have a puppet watching to give points to those who listen well.
- Some children are very good at expressive reading and you may sometimes want to choose an older child to read the story. Have them prepare the reading beforehand.

Telling a story using a video

If you have access to a television and video player, and your church holds a Performing Rights Society church licence (details from CCLI), this can be another way of telling a story. It is particularly effective if you have a big screen in your church. Watching a video occasionally, especially as part of party times, can be likened to going to the cinema with popcorn, snacks or craft activities linked to the teaching or included during the interval.

What you need: Video.
Video player and television or big screen projector.

What you do:

- Make sure that the screen is big enough for all the children to see.

- Have the children sit comfortably.
- Choose a video that is not too long or show excerpts.

Using the idea

There are plenty of good Christian videos available. Look in your Christian bookshop. We have especially enjoyed *VeggieTales* (© BigIdeas Productions Inc., Chicago), which have been well received by non-church children of all ages. Church children have often seen them before so the 8- to 12-year-old boys may not be quite so keen.

Another popular series for younger children is the *Story Keepers* by Brian Brown (© SP Media Shepherd Films Ltd) which has been shown on television. *The Miracle Maker* has been well received. This lends itself to watching in serial form, with other activities to support the teaching week by week.

It is possible to take an extract from a non-Christian video to show to the children to support your teaching. For example, we have used extracts from *Free Willy* (© Warner Brothers) to illustrate trust, care, bullying or dishonesty, and the end of *Cool Runnings* (© The Walt Disney Company) to illustrate perseverance, courage, triumphing even in defeat. *Free Willy* appeals to all ages, while *Cool Runnings* particularly appeals to the older boys.

We used extracts from *A Bug's Life* (© Disney/Pixar) to introduce our group, BUGZ, and this also gives the message of good triumphing over evil and working together as a team.

Extracts from *Prince of Egypt* (© DreamWorks International LLC) make good viewing for telling the story of Moses to older children.

Telling a story using quizzes

Quizzes are really good for introducing a story or for helping to remember the teaching. There are many ways of organising a quiz – question-and-answer, a quiz board, quiz games. Why not explore a variety of different ways that quizzes can be presented, questions designed, answers given and scores recorded? Be creative, for example using ideas from television familiar to the children in your club.

Quizzes can be used to review the content of a Bible passage or to reinforce learning taking place in other parts of the session. The technique refreshes memories and reinforces knowledge and allows the leader to check understanding and the recognition of key points. Elaborating a point after an answer is given conveys this to the whole group in a lively way.

Other quizzes may be broader in nature, covering general Bible knowledge of well-known characters and events. For more arbitrary and fun questions, you could choose obscure facts about the Bible's books, such as the name of the shortest book, or the number of books in the Old and New Testaments. For older children you could include how to spell names such as 'Abraham' and 'Leviticus'. Such trivia might seem of marginal value but, with incidental explanations, it can serve to engender interest and curiosity among the children, as well as convey a sense of the bigger picture of the Bible's scope and structure.

Designing the questions

Questions can be asked in several ways, from simple, easy-to-answer True / False options to more structured multiple-choice options, or open-ended questions requiring the player to give their own answer – potentially the hardest to answer. Another technique is to ask an open-ended question but to offer clues or hints, such as, 'It starts with the letter …' until the correct answer is forthcoming. Clues can be used at the leader's discretion, but may also depend upon the group's perception of fun versus fair play!

A rather different style of question is found in TV programmes such as *Family Fortunes.* To emulate this, you will need several possible correct answers to a question, ranked in some order of your choosing. Two players or teams respond as quickly as they can and the one with the highest scoring listed answer decides whether to try for the remainder or hand it over. If they fail to complete the remainder, the other team is given the chance to 'steal' the remaining points. Questions can be related to the theme, such as the one we used on water:

Name seven things you can do with water:

Baptise (7)
Drink (6)
Wash / Clean (5)
Swim / Sports (4)
Cook (3)
Fish (2)
Sail (1)

Of course, there may be other valid answers, but only those listed by the quiz setter score points. The scorer or the whole audience can make the noise associated with a wrong answer as used on the TV show.

Answering the questions

The way answers are given will depend partly on the type of questions posed and the nature of the group. Although individuals could be asked in turn, some could find this intimidating. Forming teams is more common. These could play competitively, divided according to existing groupings within the club, or according to sections of the room, such as left versus right. Gender (not very 'PC' but still popular) and home district are other possibilities, but may have implications for increasing rivalry rather than unity.

Each member of the team can take a turn to answer questions (with or without conferring, as appropriate), or a spokesperson could be nominated. The latter has the advantage of avoiding embarrassment to individuals who don't know the answers as well as encouraging co-operation and social skills. Some games lend themselves to a more lively method, such as calling out an answer as quickly as possible, ahead of the opponents.

Some game shows eliminate participants but if this method is adopted, the children may no longer feel involved and lose interest, which presents its own problems.

Timing the answers

For added fun – or tension – answering time can be limited to a certain number of seconds. This can be achieved audibly by an individual 'counting down' the final ten seconds, or by playing a tape of the sounds of a drum rhythm leading into a drum roll as the final seconds arrive. Ask a musician with a drum machine or a keyboard if they can create a tape for you, similar to the sequence used by the TV programme *Countdown*.

A more visual method can sometimes be achieved by using an old clock with a sturdy second hand and an overhead projector. A second-hand timer from a school laboratory with a stop/start control and removable front glass might be ideal. Ask someone gifted in practical skills to attach an extension pointer to the second hand, so that it can lie flat on its back on an OHP slide, marked up as a clock face around its perimeter. When projected, the body of the clock shows as a central black area, while the extended second hand 'ticks' around the outer area.

Keeping the scores

Although keeping score is optional, it does usually give a certain 'edge' to the activity! There is endless scope for creating visual scoreboards using a flip-chart, overhead projector, wall display or even physical objects, such as blocks for a tower. The space and facilities available will influence what you can choose to do, and the atmosphere created during the playing of the quiz. You may also be able to involve another leader or helper, whose talents lie in the area of visual or practical skills, to create an interesting piece of equipment for this and for future competitive occasions.

The simplest form of scoreboard is the score sheet, either displayed on a large sheet or on OHP, using water-based markers if you want to use the slide again later. A scorer simply adds the amount to a team's column until a total is reached. Slightly more sophisticated is a score sheet showing a line of objects, or a trail, which is progressively shaded in. Alternatively, pre-cut shapes relating to the theme could be placed onto the display to track progress towards a final goal – itself relating to the theme.

Scoreboards used on TV game shows can provide ideas and, if recognisable, a sense of connection with something familiar. The Blockbusters two-way grid of hexagonal panes containing initial letters can offer contestants the chance to control which question they try and, at the same time, have a clue about the answer. (Have several possible questions available for each set of initials, in case the grid is needed more than once or questions of varying difficulty are required.)

For a more space-consuming and active method, try the Strike It Lucky (Strike It Rich) model which uses rows of screens, each with one of three displays which, when revealed, state: 'Go on', 'Question', or 'Hot Spot', where a player must stop until answering the next question. For this you will need at least one clear wall, with room for two or more rows of about ten pieces of card, A4 size or larger, one row above the other, in front of which the players pass along towards the finish. Alternatively, a row of chairs could become the 'pathway' along which scoring players proceed. (Remember to offer questions which score more than one point each, so that 'Hot Spots' can halt a player's progress.)

A final option is, of course, to use no visual display of any kind, but ask one person to keep a tally sheet until the end of each round, or even the end of the quiz, before announcing the scores. This can help to play down the significance of 'beating' the other side during the quiz and relegate the final result to 'a bit of fun' at the end.

Section Eight: **Prayer and Praise**

It is possible to praise God and to pray with non-church children. Most primary school children are used to singing in school and some also use signing for the deaf as they sing. This can give more meaning to the song, although actions also have an invaluable place. We have found that children are eager to pray when given a framework within which to do so. In fact, it can be their expectation because they are in a church group.

In asking children to praise and pray, we do have to ask ourselves the question, 'Can they in all honesty sing or say the words in this song or prayer?' We usually find that they want to pray, especially when it is their turn to choose a prayer from a children's prayer book. Spontaneous prayer is a little more challenging as they are not used to talking freely with their heavenly Father, but we have found them happy to share their prayer needs with the leaders or in small groups. One 11-year-old girl once said to us, 'If you can't talk about your problems and have people pray for you in church, where can you talk to people?'

The prayer and praise ideas in this section introduce children to creative ways of praying and praising. Some use games, percussion instruments, dance, puppets and parachutes as well as singing, writing or drawing. The objective is to encourage children to enter into prayer and praise.

Using Songs

Some children enjoy singing, others do not – same as grown ups, really! What can matter is the song chosen. With older children it needs to have 'street cred'. That's where songwriters like Doug Horley, Jim Bailey and Ishmael come into their own. They write songs which really pick up on the music style of today. They also produce excellent recorded music to sing along with – look on the shelves in your local Christian bookshop. Many have listening posts where you can listen to the CDs and decide which will best suit the children in your club.

What you need: Musician(s) or CD player and suitable CDs.
Acetates and OHP.

What you do:

Play new songs earlier in the session, and maybe over a few weeks, so that the children become familiar with the tunes. Choose a special song that you can use to gather the children. We use 'gather music' or 'call music' to get the children together. This is always the same. In our case we chose the Muppet theme tune.

CDs are easier to use than tapes as the track can more instantly be found. Go for the full CD rather than a backing track, as this gives a fuller and more satisfying sound for the children to sing along to.

Keep the pace going and have an expectation that the children will join in. Singing to CDs makes it sound as if there are loads of people singing. You may want the children to do actions or dance in Doug Horley's 'funky' style. (See idea 90 for more on this.)

Non-church children

Can the children really tell Jesus that they love him? Can they really tell him that they are following him? You may want to choose songs based on Scripture that do not compromise ethnic or religious backgrounds. However, in a church group, singing 'Jesus focused' songs should be expected by the children and their parents. Some of the children will be able to sing songs to Jesus, rather than just about him, and you may feel that such songs are supporting the aim of the group.

Using puppets

These two ideas look at how puppets can be used to lead the singing or prayer time. The puppet becomes the 'praise leader' or the 'prayer leader' and enthusiastically sets the scene.

What you need: Puppets.
CD player.
CD of your choice. (CDs are easier to cue for the songs than tapes but songs on tapes can be used.)
Acetates and OHP.

1. Puppets lead the singing

What you do:

- Gather the children together, maybe using ‘gathering music’ or ‘call music’. This keeps the session fast-moving as the children respond to the music and get ready for what’s coming next. Be ready to start as soon as they are sitting down.
- Have the puppet ‘set the scene’ as the praise leader by enthusiastically calling the children to singing, and start the CD.
- Have the puppet encourage the children to sing more loudly, quietly, enthusiastically, etc.

2. Puppets in prayer

What you do:

- *Spontaneous prayers.* The prayer puppet provides the opportunity for the children to pray their own prayers. The children feel secure because the prayer puppet is encouraging them. The children could be given an object to pass round so that they know when to pray. (See also idea 94.)
- *Prepared prayers.* Earlier in the session the children would have written down their prayers, or some children could have chosen prayers from a book of children’s prayers. (See also idea 93.) Now is the time to pray them. These can be read, bounced (see idea 89), flown (idea 97) or placed in balloons (idea 100).
- The prayer puppet can lead the children in a prayer activity. The children write down their prayers and then either say them or place them somewhere, for example in a basket, on blue fabric representing a river, on a cross.

Using percussion instruments

Even older children enjoy playing in the band and accompanying the singing with instruments. Another challenge for them is to tap out the beat with a pencil, or drum out a rhythm with their hands.

Percussion instruments

Using the idea

A good song for younger children is *'What noise shall we make?'* by Lucy East (© 1995 Thankyou Music) on the *CD God's Wonderful World/Thank You God For Snails* (Julia Plaut, Children's Ministry) This can be linked to a craft activity where instruments are made ready for the praise time or singing time. The children enjoy using instruments that they have made but, as the weeks go by, you may want them to just pick one out of the basket for speed, unless their own instruments are kept in their teams for ease of handing out. It may, therefore, be a good idea to explain that these are being made for everyone to use.

1. Making shakers

What you need: Two clean plastic pots of the same style (eg yoghurt pots) for each child.
Sticky tape.
Scissors.
Pasta.

What you do:

- Give each child two pots with open ends that will fit together.
- Place some pasta inside one pot.
- Stick the pots together with the sticky tape.
- Decorate if liked with stickers or adhesive shapes.
- The pot is now ready to shake.

2. Drumming

Ever wanted to be a drummer in the band? This is not as easy as you might think and can be a good challenge for older children.

What you need: One or two pencils for each child.
A table to sit round.

What you do:

- Sit the children round the table.
- Introduce the idea of beat and experiment with different rhythms.
- Play a song with children beating out the rhythm.
- Talk about the rhythm – is it 4⁄4 time or 3⁄4 time?

3. Using hands

Tapping, clapping, rubbing, drumming of hands on arms, legs, tummies, etc can all make fun supporting sounds, either as part of a story or while playing music or singing a song. Experiment with the different sounds that can be made by any of the following:

- Tapping fingers together: one, two, three or four.
- Rubbing hands together.
- Clapping hands, feet, wrists.
- Drumming with hands on legs, tummies, arms.

Bible link

The storm on the lake (Luke 8:22–25).

Using the idea

As you tell the story, the children provide the sound effects. For example:

*One day, Jesus and his friends were sailing across the lake in a boat. Jesus was really tired and he soon fell asleep. Then it began to rain. (*Tap fingers together.) *The rain got heavier* (Begin with one, then two, three and four fingers as the rain begins to fall more heavily) ... *and heavier.*

*A storm was coming. (*Hands clapping softly then getting louder and louder.)

The boat began to rock as it was tossed about in the storm. (Hands drumming on legs / tummies / arms. This can happen all at once as the children choose what they want to do.)

The disciples shouted, 'Wake up, Jesus! Wake up! We're going to drown!' Jesus woke up and told the wind and the rain to be quiet. The storm stopped and all was quiet. (Get the children to listen for the quiet as the tapping, clapping, drumming comes to an end.)

This story could also be dramatised by some of the children while the others provide the sound effects.

Praise with a parachute

The children usually get really excited when they see the parachute and their first thoughts will be playing with it. It is a good idea therefore to play some games before you use the parachute as a focus for praise.

What you need: A parachute.
CD or tape player with suitable CD or tape.

What you do:

- The children stand round the parachute.
- Choose a suitable song and have the children move the parachute in response to the words, for example:
  - Lift: lift the parachute.
  - March or walk: all face the same direction and hold the parachute with

one hand. Change hands to change direction.
- Clap: let go of the parachute, clap, catch the parachute again.
- Heaven: lift high.
- Earth: take low.
- Praise: lift high or run round.
- Sing praises: lift the parachute or gently wave in time with the music.
- Glory: mushroom the parachute.

Other movements can include passing the parachute through the hands in one direction and then the other. Or to represent turning from sin and wrong doing, hold the parachute with one hand, turn away from parachute and grasp hold of it with the empty hand, then lean outwards.

Using the idea
Use the parachute to accompany the song *'Lord you put a tongue in my mouth'* (Ishmael © 1983 Thankyou Music).

Verse 1: Walk round singing.

Verse 2: Raise the parachute up to mushroom on 'raise to you', then let it come down. Build up the rhythm of lifting and dropping to match the words.

Verse 3: Gently move the parachute up and down as the children jig about with their feet.

Prayer with a parachute

What you need: A play parachute.
CD or tape player.
Suitable CD or tape.

What you do:

- Talk to the children about being still to think about God.
- Ask those who would like to lie under the parachute to put up their hands.
- Those children are numbered round the parachute either 1 or 2.
- Those who don't want to go underneath hold the parachute.
- Children numbered 2 go underneath the parachute and lie down. Number 1 children help to hold the parachute.
- Ask the children to lie still and to keep their head, legs and arms on the floor.
- The children holding the parachute gently move it up and down, floating it above the children lying on the floor.
- Ask the children on the floor to think about God's love and care.

- Play the song *'Jesus, touch me now'* by Alan Price (© 1996 Daybreak Music Ltd). After verse 1 call the number 2 children out from under the parachute. Ask them to hold the parachute for the children numbered 1.
- Invite the children numbered 1 to go under the parachute and to lie down while the music continues to play.
- Call the children out and have them sit round the parachute while you conclude in prayer.

Saying 'sorry' with a parachute

What you need: A parachute.
A CD player and gentle music.

What you do:

Explain to the children that doing wrong things makes us 'dirty' in God's sight – like dirty washing. Ask them if they would like to go in the 'washing machine' and be made clean again. You can ask for specific things the children want to say 'sorry' for, or keep the idea general.

Play 'Washing Machine' as follows:

- Children stand around parachute.
- Number the children alternately 1 or 2.
- Number 1s hold the parachute.
- Number 2s go under the parachute and lie on the floor.
- Number 1s control the washing machine.
- Number 2s are the dirty washing.

- Number 1s switch on the washing machine, making suitable water running noises.
- Add the washing powder or liquid.
- Wash by shaking the parachute.
- Spin by passing the parachute through hands as quickly as possible.
- Dry by gently moving the parachute up and down.
- Accompany all this with the appropriate noises.
- When washing is clean and dry, change over.
- Finish by playing some gentle music as you move the parachute slowly up and down and give thanks for God's forgiveness.

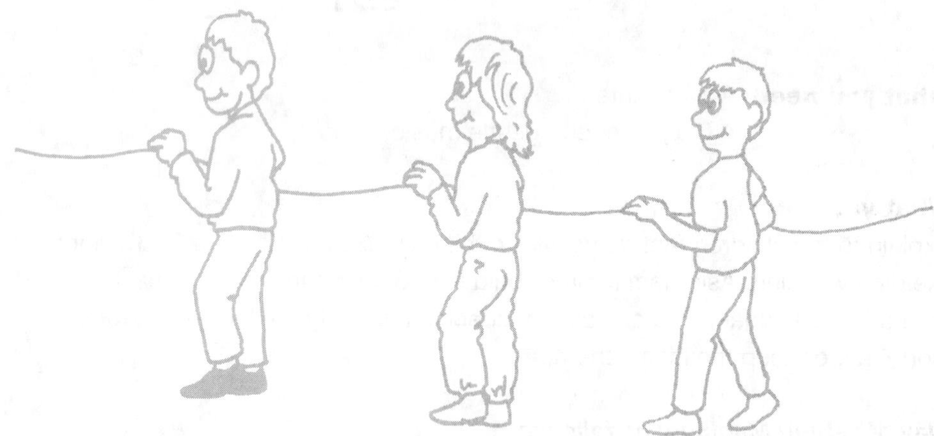

Bounce or roll a prayer

A visual way of 'sending' prayers to Jesus. This can be used in two ways – by bouncing or by rolling. Both are fun prayer activities.

What you need: A small, lightweight ball, a piece of paper and a pencil for each child.
A parachute or a king-size sheet.

What you do:

- Give out small pieces of paper and pencils to the children.
- Ask the children to write down, for example:
  - something they would like to thank God for;
  - something they would like to say 'sorry' to God for;
  - something they would like to ask God for;
  - a person they would like to pray for;

  - a country they would like to pray for;
  - a school teacher or activity they would like to pray for.
- Give each child a lightweight ball.
- Use sticky tape to attach the paper to the ball.
- Sit on the floor in a circle.
- Roll the balls across the circle.
- The children reach for a ball near them.
- When all children have a ball, read out in turn what is written, as a prayer.
- Alternatively bounce the balls on the parachute and, when all the balls are off the parachute, mushroom the parachute as you say 'Amen'.

If preferred the children can write on their piece of paper and bounce the screwed up paper on the parachute.

Using dance

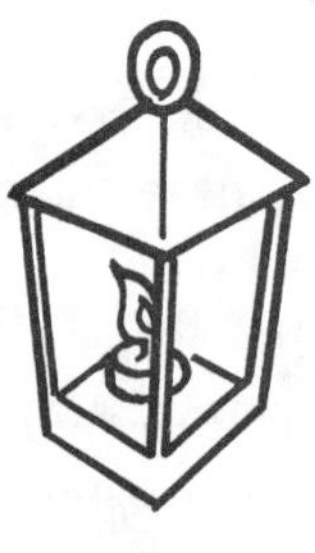

Actions are an accepted way of accompanying songs and dance is not too dissimilar. Dance can take many forms, from the 'free' dance of moving to the beat to more expressive dance – moving in a dance-like way to interpret the words of the song.

Many children will be used to doing this in school, either to music or to spoken words or poems. Choreographing a dance takes time and may suit a dance workshop, which also allows choice. The children who are not so enthusiastic about dance don't have to do it. However, the dance drama in idea 79 was done by all the children in our club and they worked out their dances in their teams.

Some songs come with suggestions for dance or actions. Duggie Dug Dug's *Funky Action Songs* videos/DVDs are available from Children's Ministry for leaders to teach dances to accompany his songs.

Marie Bensley has produced books which contain choreographed dances for use with children. These can be obtained from Kingdom Dance Resources Limited.

Using the idea

We performed a dance with a difference, using candles to accompany the song *'The Light of Christ'* by Donald Fishel (© 1974 Word of God Music). Children enjoy using candles and, although this dance may seem out of character for a children's club, we found it worked well. An Asian boy offered to take the part of 'the Light of Christ' and we presented it in church just before Christmas, when we invited parents to come and watch.

What you need: Nightlights or similar candles.
Glasses or small jars.
Blu-tack.

What you do:

- Give each child a glass or lantern with a nightlight candle Blu-tacked to the bottom. (Practise with unlit candles until everyone knows what they are doing!)
- Play the music and ask the children to gently move their candle to it.
- Group children into groups of five or seven. One child takes the role of 'the Light of Christ'.

Chorus: A single figure enters as the Light of Christ, carrying a lantern. He walks to the centre of the dance area and lifts lantern high.

Chorus repeat: Other children enter, carrying lanterns. These children walk to their places which are marked with masking tape on the floor.

Verse 1: Children gently move their glasses round in front of them in a circle. This can be a vertical circle or a horizontal circle.

Chorus: The Light of Christ character lifts lantern. The other children kneel and lift their glass up towards the Light of Christ.

Verse 2: The Light of Christ holds his lantern in front of him. The other children stand or kneel to make a cross with the lights. (It is possible!)

Chorus: Repeat as before.

Verse 3: The Light of Christ walks forward and round behind the other children while the other children first turn inwards to face each other, hiding their lights from any audience, and then from the darkness they move their lights out again as the Light of Christ walks into their midst.

Chorus: The Light of Christ walks through the audience, the other children follow and hold up their lights at the end as the song and the dance finish.

Using flags and ribbons

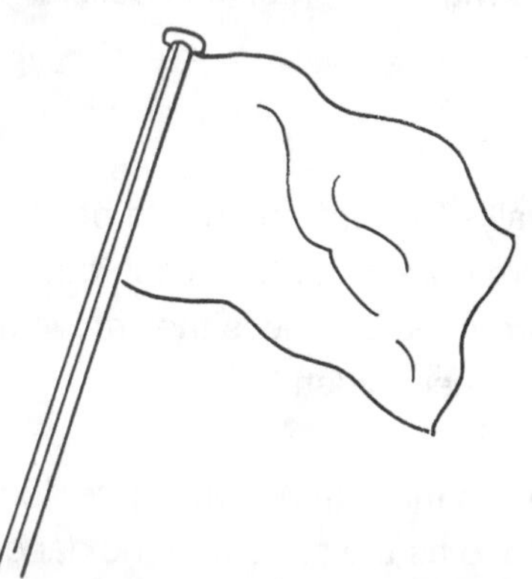

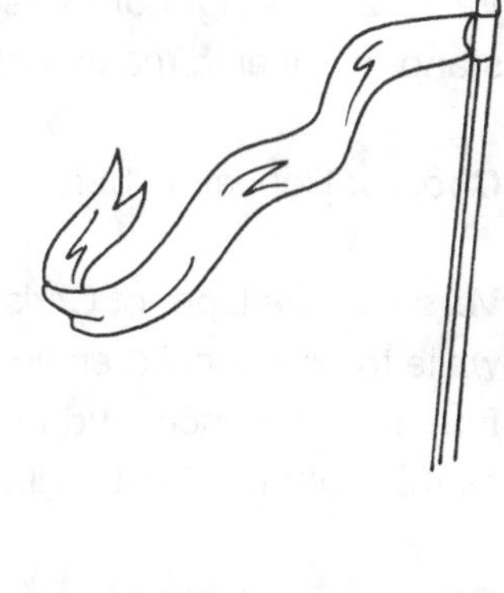

Children enjoy using flags and ribbons to accompany songs. Remember that they take up a lot of space, so make sure the children are spread out and have room to use their flags safely.

What you need: A flag or ribbon for each child.

What you do:

- Give each child a flag or a ribbon.
- Teach the children how to use the flag.
  - Move flags in a figure of eight in front of the body.
  - Wave flags above head.
  - Turn round with the flag held high.
  - Thrust flag high.
  - Thrust flag forwards.

- Walk forwards with flag, thrusting it forwards.
- Slash downwards with flag.

Using the idea

This is a suggestion for using flags for the song *'We want to see Jesus lifted high'* by Doug Horley (© 1993 Thankyou Music).

Start with flags pointing towards the ground.

Verse 1:

We want to see: lift flag up
A banner: wave to and fro.
That all men: turn around.
He is the way: thrust flag up.

Chorus:

Wave flag in front of body, gradually lifting it higher and higher.

Verse 2:

Step by step… little by little: walk forwards, thrusting flag forwards.
Every prayer: hold hands together as in prayer around the stick.
Strongholds come: move flag up and then down with strong, slashing movement.

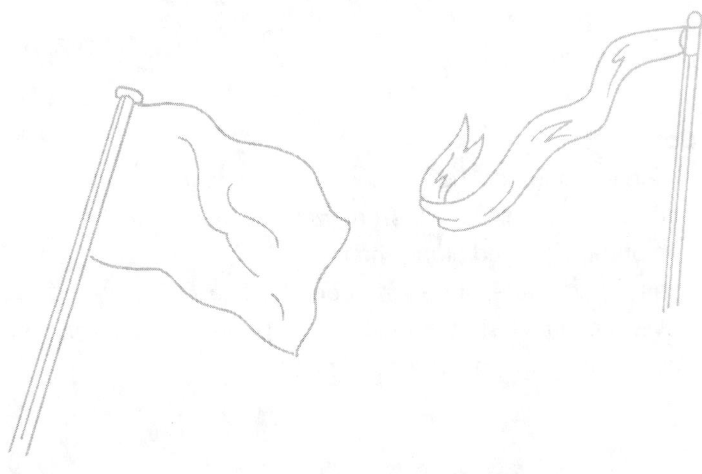

Using rap

Rap is a good way to pray, to memorise a Bible verse or to remember a Bible truth.

What you do:

- Children stand in a line holding:
  - the shoulder of the person in front with one hand;
  - a piece of rope passed along the line;
  - a rolled up parachute, sheet or piece of fabric.
- As they move, the leader shouts the line of a prayer, a Bible verse or some Bible truth in rap and the children echo back.

Using the idea

You could try a simple rap based on Psalm 150. Get the beat going and then fit the words to it. For example:

1. Praise the Lord with dancing, with dancing, with dancing.
   Praise the Lord with dancing.
   Psalm one five oh verse four.

2. Give thanks to the Lord at all times, at all times, at all times.
   Give thanks to the Lord at all times
   For this is the will of the Lord.

Using prayer books

We have found that, surprisingly, non-church children really seem to like choosing a prayer from a book. Reading the prayer gives them security that the words they are using will be all right.

What you need: A selection of children's prayer books.

What you do:
Let the children take turns each week to choose and read a prayer. You will need time beforehand for the child to choose and practise the prayer or, if you have more than one book, you could let the child take the book home to choose and practise. The advantage of this is that it can involve the families, especially if you send a letter of explanation home with the child. The disadvantage is the child may forget to bring the book back for the next meeting! Having more than one copy of the book can overcome this problem.

The prayer can be read at the end of the story time or at the end of the session. If you choose the end of the session, you may find the children are calmer if they are sitting on chairs, possibly in a circle if you use circle time to conclude your meetings.

Pass the Beanie

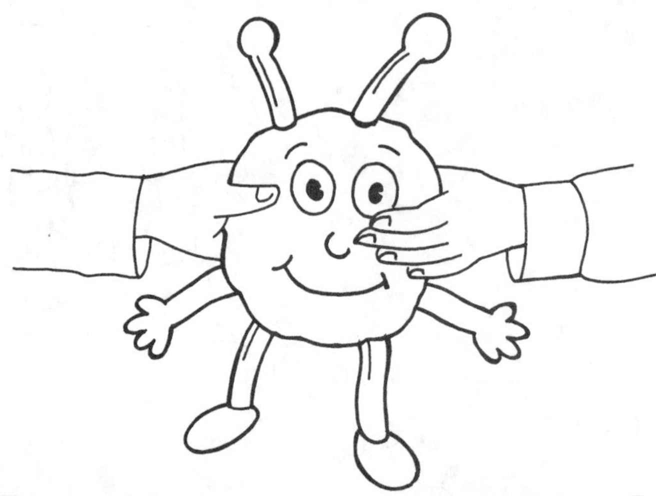

This enables each child to have the opportunity to pray or to share news if they want to. Passing an object helps all the children know whose turn it is. We have also found that holding an object has given the children confidence to speak – especially when the object is soft.

What you need: An object such as a Beanie toy.

What you do:

- Children sit in a circle.
- Pass the object round the circle.
- The children are invited to say a prayer, either out loud or in their head, when they have the toy.
- When they have finished their prayer, or if they don't want to pray, they pass the object to the next child.
- This continues until all have had a turn.

This idea can also be used for sharing news.

Prayer partners

Non-church children can do this too.

What you need: Paper and pencil for each child.

What you do:

- Give each child a piece of paper and a pencil.
- Ask them to write down something that they would like prayer for – for example, a test at school, a visit to the dentist, to play well in a sports match, etc.
- Then ask the children to join up with a partner, or with the child next to them if they are in a circle. You may have to pair them off to make this work out.
- The children then swap papers and say a prayer like, 'Lord Jesus, please help (name of child) with (read off the paper).'

ADDITIONAL IDEA

Another idea is to pass a Beanie toy or similar around. When they have the toy, the children say a prayer of blessing for the child next to them, eg: 'Lord Jesus, please bless (name).'

Praying for the Family

This idea is particularly suitable for younger children.

What you need: A piece of paper or card cut into a house shape for each child. Crayons or felt pens.

What you do:

- Give each child a house-shaped piece of paper.
- Ask the children to draw in the windows and doors of their house.
- Then they draw members of their family looking out of the windows.
- A simple sentence could be written on the roof: 'Lord Jesus, please bless my family.'
- Colour in if desired.

Using the idea

You can encourage the children to be thinking especially about each member of their family as they draw them. They can say 'thank you' to God for them, and if they are poorly, they can ask God to help them to feel better. At the end, all say together, 'Lord Jesus, please bless my family.' You may want to say this and have the children repeat the words after you.

Flying prayers

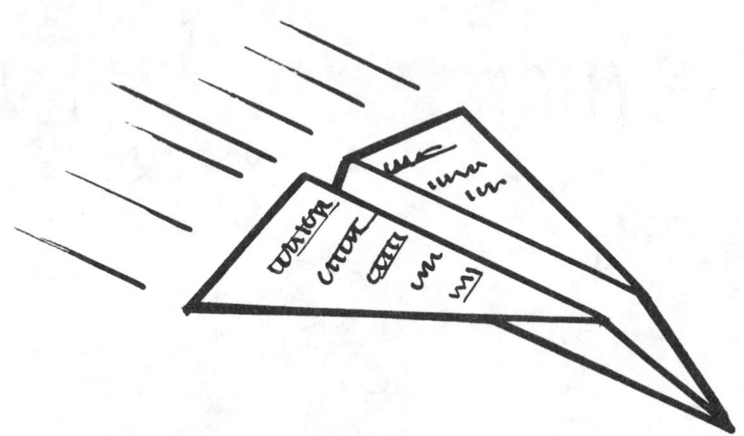

Why not fly your prayer to Jesus? Be prepared for the flying of the prayers to be active, noisy and excitable! Have plenty of leaders around to help the children to follow directions. This is great fun, not just in children's groups but in all-age services too. This idea is best suited to children who can write and read independently.

What you need: A4 size piece of paper for each child.
Pen or pencil for each child.

What you do:

- Ask the children to make a paper aeroplane. I think most children would know how to do this, but if not:
  - Take the A4 piece of paper and fold it in half vertically. Flatten out.
  - Fold the two top corners to the centre fold to make a triangle.

  - Fold each corner again into a triangle to make a sharp point at the top of the paper.
  - Fold in half along the already folded vertical.
  - Fold out the wings to form a body.
  - Your aeroplane is now ready to fly!
- Children write their prayer on the wing of the plane.
- When the children have written what will usually be a one word prayer, they get ready to fly their planes by holding them high. On the command… FLY.
- Children run to pick up a plane and after the leader has said an introductory prayer eg 'Father God, we pray for…', the children say what's written on the plane.
- The planes can be flown again.
- At the end of the 'flying time', say 'Amen'.

Using the idea

Flying prayers can be used to pray for many different people and situations, particularly 'thank you' prayers and prayers for other countries. If using to pray for other countries, you may want to talk about travelling to these other countries by plane.

The children could do the following:

- Pray for children in another country (write name of country on wing of plane).
- Pray for friends (write friend's name).
- Pray for school (write name of school).
- Pray for an end to fighting or famine or to ask for rain / no rain, or food.
- Say 'thank you' prayers (eg for sunshine, your help, toys, friends, outing, etc).
- Say 'sorry' prayers (eg for being cross, stealing, bullying, etc).

The leader will say the appropriate introductory prayer sentence:

- 'Lord Jesus, thank you for our friends. Please bless …' (name friends).
- 'Dear Lord, we pray for the teachers and children in these our schools' (name schools).
- 'We pray for (or please bless) the people in these countries' (name countries).

At the end of the 'flying time', say 'Amen' together.

Prayer consequences

This idea can be used for 'thank you' and 'sorry' prayers and praying for others. It can also be used for all three at once. This is a prayer game for older children who can read and write independently.

What you need: A piece of paper and a pencil for each child.

What you do:

- The children write down one thing that they would like to say 'thank you' to God for. The paper is folded over and passed to the next child.
- The next child writes down another thing, folds the paper over and passes on. Continue for five or six things.
- At the end, the papers are opened. Give children time to read through the list.
- Lead the children in prayer. For example: 'Thank you, Lord, for' (children read through list on their sheet of paper).

- Together say 'Amen'.

Using the idea

This idea can also be used for 'sorry' prayers and for praying for others. The 'sorry' prayers need to be kept general as others will be reading them. We are saying 'sorry' as a group for the things that people do that do not please God.

When praying for others the children write down the name of their school; a country they've heard of in the news or would like to pray for; a friend they would like to invite to the group; or a member of their family. Fold the paper over each time as in the idea above, and introduce each prayer idea with your own prayer. For example:

- 'Lord Jesus, we pray for our schools' (all say name of school on their paper).
- 'Lord, we pray for the people in these countries' (say countries).
- 'We thank you for our friends. We would like these friends to have fun with us at (name of group).'
- 'We pray for our families, especially (name).'
- 'Please bless all the people we have prayed for. In Jesus' name. Amen.'

Folding a cross

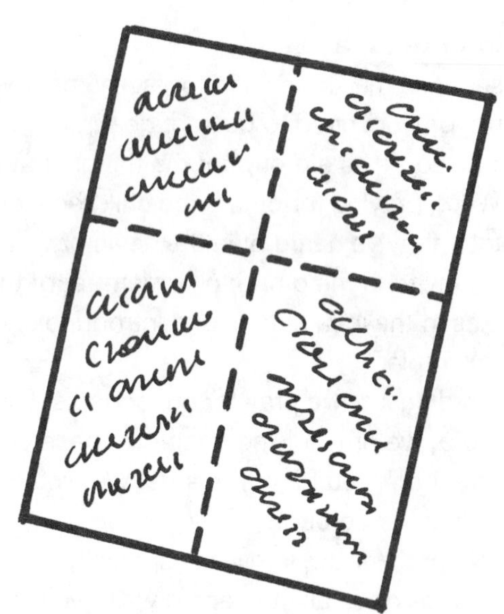

This idea is a good way to illustrate the bringing of people and situations to the cross of Jesus. It is a quiet, reflective way of praying, best suited to older children who can write independently, but it can be used with younger children as pictures can be drawn. You may like to have instrumental music playing in the background to give a beginning and end to the prayer time.

What you need: A piece of A6 paper for each child.
A pen or pencil for each child.
A cross.
A basket.

What you do:

- Hold paper by short side.
- Fold paper lengthways.
- Open and fold top short edge to middle of paper.
- Open.
- The children write the names of people, schools or situations as directed for prayer.
- The papers are then placed in a basket under the cross as their prayers.
- Either leave the papers in the basket as 'personal' requests to God, or draw them out and pray them aloud for all to hear and say 'Amen'.

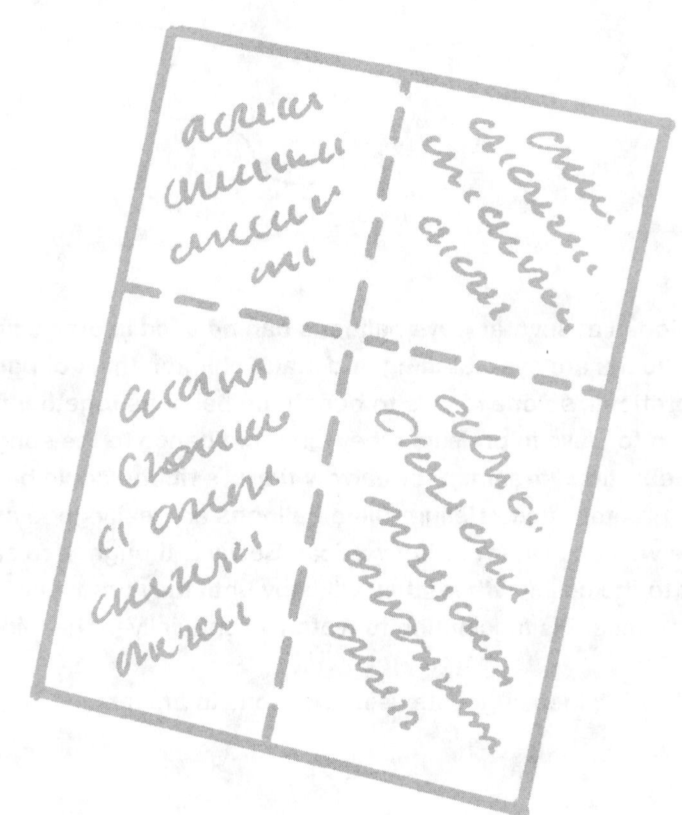

Using balloons

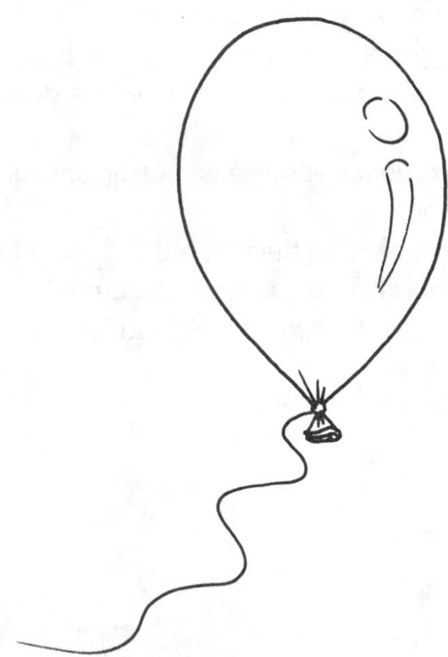

This idea looks at several ways balloons can be used in praise and prayer. Balloons are eye-catching and make children think of parties and celebrations, so one idea is to bunch the balloons together for the children to wave in praise as they sing and dance to the songs.

For celebration, streamers or narrow florist's ribbon could be added for greater effect. Helium-filled balloons are really good as they move well and return to the vertical. Beware, though. If released they float to the ceiling where they will stay until they gradually lose gas. Their descent is fascinating to watch – especially in the mid-air stage!

The following idea suggests using balloons in prayer.

What you need: A balloon for each child.
A piece of paper and pencil for each child.
A pump to inflate balloons.

What you do:

- The children each write a praise or thank you message onto a piece of paper which is then pushed inside their balloon.
- Blow up the balloons.
- The messages can then be bounced to Jesus by keeping the balloons in the air.

Using the idea

Prayer can be quiet and reverent but it can also be joyous. This way of praying is no less meaningful, for the Lord knows our hearts. Praying is communicating with God, and the children are communicating by using their energy to bounce their prayers to God. They could also write their message on the outside using permanent felt pens.

Use this idea also to support the teaching. The words 'God cares', 'Jesus loves', 'Jesus is born' (Christmas), 'Jesus is alive' (Easter) written on the balloons will help the children to remember the teaching.

For memorising a Bible verse, write one word of the verse on each balloon and then have the children stand in a line making up the verse. The verse could then be said out loud.

Balloons can also be used in saying 'sorry' to God, with one word on each balloon, eg: greed, hatred, selfishness, cheating, lying, etc. When everyone is ready, pray a 'saying sorry' prayer and burst the balloons.

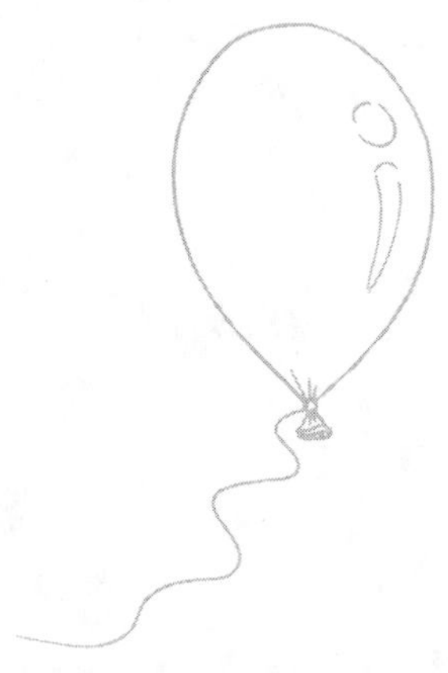

PART THREE

Flags and Ribbons

Flags and ribbons can make a declaration. In battle, flags show whose side we are on (see Numbers 1:50—2:2, 17, 31, 34). The colours are symbolic. For example, gold for majesty; purple for kingship; blue for the water of life; silver for the Holy Spirit; red for Jesus (his death, sacrifice, grace, our salvation); green for healing, rest, life; yellow for glory, light, celebration; black for sin and death.

Children usually enjoy using flags and ribbons. They need to be taught how to use them safely so that they don't hurt each other or tie themselves up in knots. Think about how you are going to give them out and collect them in. Consider a policy where children are not encouraged to play with the flags and ribbons when they are not being used in the group. A suggested policy is available from Kingdom Resources Limited. They can also supply ready-made flags and ribbons.

Using flags and ribbons safely

Ask the children to watch the flag or the ribbon and to be careful about others near to them. Check that the children have enough space to move them safely. When children are using flags, remember that the top of the flag may be at eye level for adults!

A figure-of-eight movement will prevent the flag from wrapping round the cane or the ribbon around the stick. The power and strength of the movement will be determined by the song, as will the variation of the movements, and space required.

There are many ways of moving with flags and ribbons. For more information, contact Kingdom Dance Resources Limited or the Christian Dance Fellowship of Britain.

Making flags

For each flag you will need a piece of lightweight material 60cm by 50cm and a length of cane 75cm long.

- Take a piece of lightweight material in the colour of your choice.
- Turn over the shorter edge and sew up to make a slot for the cane to slide into.
- Sew up one end of the slot.
- Slide in the cane.
- Finally, secure the flag to the cane using sticky fixers inside the slot.

Making ribbons

You will need a length of double-sided satin ribbon, approximately 3m long and 5cm wide; a piece of lightweight dowelling, approximately 30cm long; a swivel (obtainable from a fishing shop); a small metal ring, and a small closed hook.

- The simplest way is to take the ribbon and hem the short ends. Folding one end back on itself by 50cm will give a better flow as it provides weight at that end; the sides of the folded end will also need to be sewn.
- Sew the ring to one end (if your ribbon is folded back, choose the folded end).
- Attach this to the swivel.
- Screw a closed hook into the top of the dowelling.
- Attach the swivel to the hook.

Parachutes

A parachute is a really useful piece of equipment. It is fun to play with and has so many uses in a midweek group, from games and stories to prayer and praise. As with all activities, some thought needs to be given to safe play. Below are some safety rules you may want to adopt. As you begin to use a parachute with your children, you may want to add to these as you observe their response to its use.

Using a parachute

When first using the parachute, we agree the safety procedure by talking to the children about the parachute:

- When using a parachute with loops along the edge, we ask the children to keep their hands out of the loops. We ask them to tell us why.
- We ask them not to put their heads through the hole in the middle. Again, we ask them why.
- We have them take their shoes off for games played under or on top of the parachute.
- We roll the edge of the parachute in a little for a better grip.

As we use the parachute, all of us are responsible for the well-being of ourselves and others. You may want to give everyone permission to shout 'Stop!' if they feel the situation is unsafe. The children should always stop on your command. If you need to stop an activity for safety reasons, explain why. Praise positive behaviour.

Check that the room is suitable for what you are planning to do. Consider the suitability of the space and the floor surface. Check too that the parachute is in good condition. Any small tears can be repaired. Some parachutes come with repair kits.

Where to buy

One supplier of parachutes is a company called SeamStress Ltd. SeamStress Ltd call their parachutes playchutes because they are made specially for play. This makes them more colourful and easier to use. SeamStress Ltd also supply booklets covering many topics including *Playchute Games, Environmental Games and Playchutes in Christian Teaching.* They can be contacted at:
SeamStress Ltd, 23 Banbury Road, Byfield, Northants NN11 6XJ.
Website: www.playchutes.com   Email: info@playchutes.com

Play Dough Recipe

Play dough is really useful to have available. It can be used to make models as well as with shape cutters and play dough 'machines'. It is a great favourite with all ages because it is so easy to handle. The following recipe will make enough play dough for six children.

What you need: 400g (16oz) flour
200g (8oz) salt
30g (1oz) cream of tartar
30ml (2tbs) cooking oil
600ml (1 pint) water
Food colouring
Flavouring (optional)
Glitter (optional)

What you do:

1. Put the flour, salt and cream of tartar into a larger saucepan.
2. Add food colouring.
3. Add flavouring (optional). Flavouring the play dough adds another dimension to it but may also make it smell good enough to eat. Tell the children it is not!
4. Add water, stirring in well.
5. Heat the pan on a low to medium heat, stirring all the time, until the mixture thickens and moves from the side of the pan.

6. Turn onto a floured board and, when cool enough to handle, knead until the dough is smooth and elastic. Glitter can be added at this stage, if required.
7. When completely cool, the play dough can be stored in a sealed container, in a cool place, for some time.

Using the idea

Suggested uses can be found in ideas 12–14. In addition flavoured play dough can be used in games to guess the smell as well as to appreciate the gift of smell. Different coloured play dough is enjoyable for making more colourful and creative models. If modelling clay is not available for idea 14, different coloured play dough can be substituted.

Resources

Books

Bensley, Marie, *Children's Dances* (Kingdom Dance Resources Limited).

Copsey, Kathryn, *Here's One I Made Earlier* (Scripture Union, 1998).

Dyer, Jan, *100 Creative Prayer Ideas for Children* (Kingsway, 1999).

Dyer, Jan, *Parachute for the Puppet Team and Children's Ministry* (One Way UK, 2005).

Hopwood, Dave, *Telling Tales* (CPAS, 1997).

Hopwood, Dave, *Telling More Tales* (CPAS, 1998).

Mortimer, Jonathan, *See What I Mean* (CPAS, 1998).

Neilands, Lynda, *50 Bible Dramas for Children* (Kingsway, 2005)

Neilands, Lynda, *50 Five-Minute Stories* (Kingsway, 1996, 2006).

Neilands, Lynda, *50 Stories for Special Occasions* (Kingsway, 1998).

Orme, Christine, *Here's Another One I Made Earlier* (Scripture Union, 2000).

Parry, Alan, *Dangerous Journey* (Candle Publishing, 1994).

Pinchbeck, Lesley, *Theme Games 1* (Scripture Union, 1993).

Pinchbeck, Lesley, *Theme Games 2* (Scripture Union, 2003)

Powerpack, *Play on Words* (Powerpack Ministries, 1997).

Price, Sue, *100 Simple Craft Ideas for Children* (Kingsway, 1998).

Relf, Sue, *100 Instant Children's Talks* (Kingsway, 1994, 2006).

SeamStress Ltd, *Playchute Games* (SeamStress Ltd, 1995).

SeamStress Ltd, *Playchutes in Christian Teaching* (SeamStress Ltd, 1999).

Bibles and Bible stories

The Adventure Bible – New International Version (Hodder & Stoughton, 1989).

God's Story (Kingsway, 1999).

Hermie and Friends (Tommy Nelson Publishers Inc, 2004).

Kidsbible.com (Tommy Nelson Publishers Inc, 2001).

The Lion Children's Bible (Lion Publishing).

The Lion Encyclopaedia of the Bible (Lion Publishing).

Hartman, Bob, *Angels, Angels all Around* (Lion Publishing, 1995).

Hartman, Bob, *The Storyteller Bible* (Lion Publishing, 1995).

Hartman, Bob, *Bible Baddies* (Lion Publishing, 1999).

Rowlands, Avril, *Animal Tales from the Bible* (Lion Publishing, 2001).

For younger children

The Storykeepers (Paternoster Publishing, 1998).

Butterworth, Nick and Mick Inkpen, *Stories Jesus Told* (Marshall Pickering, 1996).

Music

The following songwriters and children's praise leaders produce songs suitable for non-church children's clubs. Look in your local Christian bookshop. Most bookshops now offer a 'listening facility' for you to listen to a CD and decide on its suitability for your group.

Jim Bailey

Dave Godfrey

John Hardwick

Doug Horley

Ishmael

Julia Plaut

Captain Alan Price

For puppet presentations

RPM – CDs and tapes. These can be obtained from One Way UK.

DVDs/Videos

Again, look on the shelves of your local Christian bookshop. The following are suggestions:

Angel Wars – Guardian Force Episode 1 (Children's Ministry)

Angel Wars – Guardian Force Episode 2 (Children's Ministry)

Hermie & friends (Tommy Nelson)

Hillsong Kids (Hillsong Music)

Miracle Maker (© Warner Bros).

The Story Keepers (© SP Media Shepherd Films Ltd).

Prince of Egypt (© Dreamworks International LLC).

For younger children

VeggieTales (© Big Idea Productions).

For leaders

Duggie Dug Dug's Action Songs Videos/DVDs.

Useful Addresses

Child protection
Churches' Child Protection Advisory Service,
PO Box 133, Swanley, Kent BR8 7UQ.
Website: www.ccpas.co.uk
Email: info@ccpas.co.uk

Christian copyright
Christian Copyright Licensing International Ltd,
PO Box 1339, Eastbourne, East Sussex BN21 1AD.
Website: www.ccli.co.uk
Email: info@ccli.co.uk

Dance
Christian Dance Fellowship of Britain,
National Office, 14 Brecon Drive,
Stourbridge, West Midlands DY8 4UU
Website: www.cdfb.org.uk
Email: jan.cdfb@hotmail.co.uk

Kingdom Dance Resources Limited (for flags, ribbons, ready choreographed dances and scripted dramas), Sunset Gate, St Audries, Taunton TA4 4EA.
Website: www.kingdomdance.co.uk
Email: bensley@clara.net

Dramatic Bible reading
Powerpack Resource Centre, 56 Westfield Road,
Westfield, Woking, Surrey GU22 9NG
Website: powerpackministries.co.uk
Email: info@ppcentre.co.uk

Gospel illusions
Tricks for Truth, Horse Carrs,
Shaw Clough Road, Rochdale OL12 6LG
Website: www.tricksfortruth.com
Email: office@tricksfortruth.com

Music
Children's Ministry,
26-28 Lottbridge Drove,
Eastbourne, East Sussex BN23 6NT
Website: www.childrensministry.co.uk
Email: childrensministry@kingsway.co.uk

Daybreak Music Ltd, PO Box 2848,
Eastbourne BN20 7XP
Email: info@daybreakmusic.co.uk

Duggie Dug Dug (Doug Horley),
PO Box 293, Epsom, Surrey KT19 9YE.
Website: duggiedugdug.co.uk
Email: duggiedugdug@clara.net

Ishmael,
Revelation Centre,
PO Box 58, Chichester, West Sussex PO19 8UD
Website: www.ishmaeldirect.com
Email: ishmael@ishmael.org.uk

Jim Bailey,
Kingdom Creative,
32 Normandy Road, Worthing, West Sussex BN14 7DX
Website: www.jimbailey.org
Email: info@jimbailey.org

John Hardwick,
12 Normanton Way, Histon, Cambridge CB4 9XS
Website: www.johnhardwick.org.uk
Email: johnhardwick36@hotmail.com

Captain Alan Price CA,
The Vicarage, Marple Road, Charlesworth, Glossop SK13 5DA.
Email: alan@charlesworthvicarage.wanadoo.co.uk

Parachutes

SeamStress Ltd (for playchutes and more ideas),
23 Banbury Road, Byfield, Northants NN11 6XJ.
Website: www.playchutes.com
Email: info@playchutes.com

Puppets

One Way UK, (for puppets, scripts, CDs, training and more),
Unit 6 Britten Road, Robert Court Industrial Estate,
Elgar Road South, Reading RG2 0AU
Website: www.onewayuk.com
Email: info@onewayuk.com

Mission

Tearfund,
100 Church Road, Teddington, Middlesex TW11 8QE.
Website: www.tearfund.org
Email: enquiry@tearfund.org

Toybox Charity (street children in Latin America),
PO Box 660, Amersham, Bucks HP6 5YT
Website: www.toybox.org
Email: info@toybox.org

Training

Children's Ministry,
26-28 Lottbridge Drove,
Eastbourne, East Sussex BN23 6NT.
Website: www.childrensministry.co.uk
Email: childrensministry@kingsway.co.uk

Church Pastoral Aid Society (CPAS),
Athena Drive, Tachbrook Park, Warwick CV34 6NG.
Website: www.cpas.org.uk
Email: info@cpas.org.uk

Scripture Union,
207–209 Queensway,
Bletchley, Milton Keynes MK2 2EB.
Website: www.scriptureunion.org.uk
Email: info@scriptureunion.org.uk

SCRIPTURE INDEX

Genesis

Idea Number

1 . . . . . 1, 12, 19, 21, 28
3 67
6–8 . . . . . 1, 23, 28, 35
13 3

Exodus

1 50
2:1–10 29
5 42
5:6–9 18
8 . . . . . 14, 16, 29, 42, 79
10 . . . . . 11, 14, 16, 42, 79
12 . . . . . 42, 65, 79
12:33–36 43
14 . . . . . 2, 42
16 . . . . . 34, 36, 65
33 1

Numbers

2:34 91
13:30–33 8
22:21–41 . . . . . 53, 57, 63

Deuteronomy

4:9 82

Joshua

3 2
24:15 3

Ruth

2 17

1 Samuel

Idea Number

17 . . . . . 55, 56, 68

1 Kings

17:1–6 . . . . . 36, 53, 65
17:8–16 . . . . . 36, 65
18:16–46 1

2 Kings

5 8

Psalms

23:5 26
148:13 100
149:1 83
150 92

Jeremiah

18:1–6 13

Ezekiel

1:4 1

Daniel

6 . . . . . 1, 15, 21, 23, 53, 54, 73

Jonah

. . . . . 28, 49, 77

Matthew

4:18–22 51
6:9–15 4
10:42 26

Matthew *continued*

11:16–17 68
13:1–9 39
13:24–30 60
13:44–46 . . . . 7, 66
14:3–12 41
14:14–21 28
14: 22-33 77
18:21–35 4
21:1–11 63
25:1–13 13
25:14–30 58

Mark

2:1–12 10
10:46–52 7
14:12–26 37

Luke

3:21–22 2
5:1–11 . . . . 5, 28, 29
8:22–24 . . . . 9, 85
9:10–17 21
9:28–36 1
10:30–37 . . . . 10, 17, 44
10:38–42 . . . . 3, 21, 23, 25
11:33–36 13
15 . . . . 7, 30, 35, 66
15:1–7 . . . . 15, 21, 25, 28, 53, 70
15:8–10 . . . . 18, 24, 78
15:11–31 . . . . 23, 27, 40, 74
17:11–19 17
19:1–10 18
23:26–43 21

John

Idea Number

1:4–5 . . . . 13, 90
1:35–42 . . . . 6, 51
2:1–11 . . . . 25, 30, 69
6:1–13 . . . . 5, 32, 35, 36, 65
12:1–3 . . . . 10, 25
13:12–15 25
15:16 . . . . 3, 52
21:1–14 21

Acts

1:9–11 1
12 64
27:27–44 . . . . 9, 59
28:11–16 38

1 Corinthians

3:18–23 62
9:24–25 61
12:12–31 . . . . 22, 45, 58

Galatians

3:28 22
5:22–23 33

Ephesians

4:25—5:2 46

Philippians

1:4 100

SUBJECT INDEX A–Z

Idea Number

A

Abraham .3
Adam and Eve .67
Animals .1
Apples 67
Ascension .1

B

Balaam .57, 63
Balloons .100
Bangers and mash .42
Basketball .45
Beads .24
Biscuit making .30, 35
Blind Bartimaeus .7
Body parts .58
Bread making .36, 37
Breakfast on the beach .21
Bricks .18
Bugs .11, 14, 16, 50
Buns .30, 41

C

Cake icing .30
Calling first disciples .5, 77
Caring .10, 22, 25, 28, 30
Cat and mouse .10, 49
Caterpillars .11
Christian life .46, 76
Chosen .3, 52

Idea Number

Circle games .5, 6, 7, 53, 71
Clay .13
Clothes .22, 43
Colour .3, 16, 75, 76
Creation .1, 15, 21, 35
Cross .21, 99
Crossing the Jordan .2

D

Dance .90
Drama .69, 70, 79
Daniel's lions .1, 15, 21, 23, 53, 54, 73
David and Goliath .55, 56
Difficult situations .64
Donkeys .53, 57, 63
Drumming .85

E

Egypt .11, 18, 29, 42, 79
Elijah .1, 36, 65
Eve .67

F

Family 17
Feeding 5,000 21, 28, 32, 35, 65
Fish 26, 28, 29, 59
Flags 76, 91, Part Three
Following 5, 51
Fool for God 61

Idea Number

Football 9, 45, 68
Forgiveness 4
Fruit of the Spirit 33

G

Gifts 19, 23, 25, 26, 58
Glue 11
Goliath 55, 56
Good Samaritan 10, 17, 44
Growing seeds 39

H

Hallowe'en (alternative) 13
Hands 17
Harvest 17
Herod's Party 41
Hidden objects 77
Honesty 8

J

Jeremiah 13
Jesus
  baptism 2
  Bethany 10
  Life of 76
Jewellery 24
Jonah 49, 77
Joseph 36
Joshua 8
Judging situations 57

Idea Number

K

Keep going 61

L

Lamp of the body 13
Last Supper 37
Light of Christ 13, 90
Lions 1, 5, 21, 23, 53, 54, 73
Listening to God 48
Locusts 11, 16
Lost
  – coin 7, 18, 24, 31, 35, 78
  – sheep . . 7, 15, 21, 25, 27, 35, 53, 70
  – son 7, 23, 27, 35, 40, 75

M

Manna 35, 65
Marshmallow pigs 27
Martha 10, 21, 25
Mary 10
Masks 1, 15, 27
Mats 19
Missionary link 31, 34, 97, 98
Modelling 1, 12, 13, 14
Moses 13, 29, 50, 79
Mothering Sunday 25, 28, 30
Mugs and plates 26
Mural 17

Idea Number

N

Naaman 8
Noah's Ark 1, 23, 28

O

Obstacle course 46

P

Painting a letter 20, 21
Pans 44
Paper masks . . . . .1 , 15, 27
Parachute
- in games 8, 9, 10
- in telling/reviewing stories 75, 77, 78
- in praise 86
- in prayer 87, 88, 89
- how to use . . . . Part Three
- where to buy . . . . Part Three

Paralysed man 10
Parties 30, 34, 38, 41
Parts of the body 58
Passover 37
Pebbles 23
Percussion 85
Persistent widow 36
Peter 64, 77
Picnic 32, 35
Pigs 23, 27, 40
Pizza 38
Plagues in Egypt 11, 14, 29
Play dough . . . . 12, Part Three

Idea Number

Playing games 68
Popcorn 9, 34
Potter's house 13
Prayer . . . 87, 88, 89, 93, 95, 96, 98, 100
Prodigal son 7, 23, 27, 35, 40, 75
Puppets 72, 73, 84

Q

Quizzes 74, 82

R

Races 40
Raven 36, 53
Red Sea 2, 14, 79
Relays 40
River 2, 50
Rolling a prayer 89
Rubbings 18, 19
Running away 49
Ruth 17

S

Salvation 76
Scripture 20, 47, 100
Seeds 39
Sharing 5, 30, 35, 95
Sharks 10
Shoes 44, 56
Size order 55
Snail race 57

Idea Number

Sorry 88, 97, 98, 100
Sower 39
Space flight 1
Stories:
  Bricks in Egypt 18
  Bright-eyed pigs 27
  David and Goliath 55
  Daniel in trouble 54, 73
  Down by the river 50
  Elijah and the widow 36
  Elijah fed by ravens 53
  Feeding the pigs 40
  The great escape 79
  The greedy taxman 18
  John the Baptist 41
  Lost coin 18, 78
  Lost sheep 70
  Mary and the angel 75
  Paul all at sea 59
  Peter in prison 64
  The Prodigal Son 23, 27
  The storm 85
  The wedding 69
Storm 9, 59, 85
Story review 28, 74, 77, 79, 82

T

Talents 58
Taking turns 94
Taxman 18
Teamwork 45, 58
Telling others 6

Idea Number

Ten bridesmaids 13
Ten lepers 17
Thank you 17, 96, 97
Transfiguration 1

V

Ventriloquism 72
Videos 34, 81

W

Waiting 50
Walking on the water 77
Wedding at Cana 25, 30, 38, 41, 69
Words and actions 70

Z

Zacchaeus 18

50 Bible Dramas For Children

by Lynda Neilands

ISBN – 1 84291 253 4

These tried and tested dramas will help today's youngsters engage with the Bible. Not every drama is designed to be performed by children. Some will work better when adults perform them and others are written for a mixture of adult and child performers. At the start of each drama there is an indication of who should ideally perform the script. Each drama also has an application section with explore, chat and think ideas.

50 Five Minute Stories

by Lynda Neilands

ISBN – 1 84291 277 1

You have been asked to fill the next five or ten minutes. You want something that will hold the children's attention and stay in their minds. A story that will give the adults something to think about. You need fresh ideas, parables, true stories, once-upon-a-time stories. You need this book!

100 Instant Children's Talks

by Sue Relf

ISBN – 1 84291 290 9

Children's talks are needed to fit many situations – church services, family services, school assemblies, Bible clubs, holiday clubs and missions, regular children's activities and so on. Here are 100 ideas that can be fitted into all of these. The talks are not intended to be slavishly followed; they can be adapted, embellished, shortened, developed or altered in whatever way is necessary in order to make them suitable for the age and background of the children and the situation in which the talk is to be given.

100 Worship Activities For Children

by Chris Leach

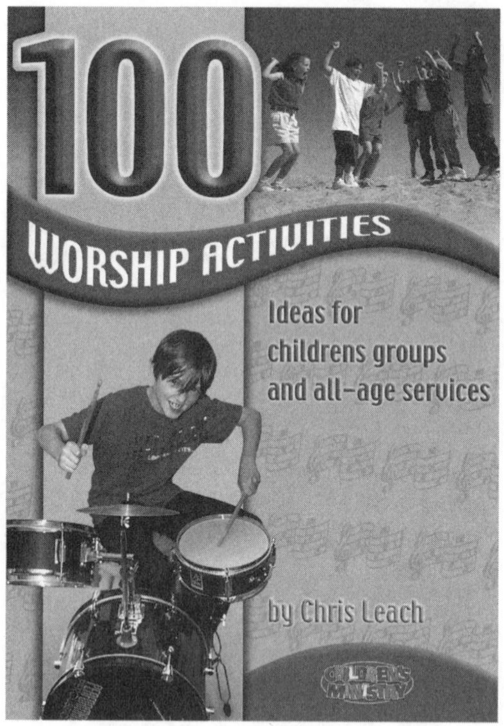

ISBN – 1 84291 297 1

This practical resource gives ideas for activities and games that illustrate the true meaning of worship, to help lead children into a deeper relationship with God. Many are also suitable for all-age services, designed to bring new life and exuberance to your church's worship time. The ideas are listed under seasons of the church year, with full theme and Scripture indexes.

100 Simple Bible Crafts

by Sue Price

ISBN – 1 84291 292 5

Many of us learn more effectively when we have something to see and something to make; when we interact rather than simply sit and listen. This collection of illustrated ideas has been specifically designed to help children learn stories and truths from the Bible in such a way that they can make them part of their lives. A useful resource that will prove invaluable to anyone who plays a part in the teaching of children.